Latent Print Processing Guide

T0383257

Latent Print Processing Guide

Stephen P. Kasper

Retired Detective, Town of Amherst Police Department
Retired Senior Crime Laboratory Analyst
Florida Department of Law Enforcement

AMSTERDAM • BOSTON • HEIDELBERG • LONDON
NEW YORK • OXFORD • PARIS • SAN DIEGO
SAN FRANCISCO • SINGAPORE • SYDNEY • TOKYO

Academic Press is an imprint of Elsevier

ELSEVIER

Academic Press is an imprint of Elsevier
125 London Wall, London EC2Y 5AS, UK
525 B Street, Suite 1800, San Diego, CA 92101-4495, USA
225 Wyman Street, Waltham, MA 02451, USA
The Boulevard, Langford Lane, Kidlington, Oxford OX5 1GB, UK

Notices
Knowledge and best practice in this field are constantly changing. As new research and
experience broaden our understanding, changes in research methods, professional practices,
or medical treatment may become necessary.

Practitioners and researchers must always rely on their own experience and knowledge in
evaluating and using any information, methods, compounds, or experiments described herein.
In using such information or methods they should be mindful of their own safety and the safety
of others, including parties for whom they have a professional responsibility.

To the fullest extent of the law, neither the Publisher nor the authors, contributors, or editors,
assume any liability for any injury and/or damage to persons or property as a matter of products
liability, negligence or otherwise, or from any use or operation of any methods, products,
instructions, or ideas contained in the material herein.

ISBN: 978-0-12-803507-8

British Library Cataloguing-in-Publication Data
A catalogue record for this book is available from the British Library

Library of Congress Cataloging-in-Publication Data
A catalog record for this book is available from the Library of Congress

For information on all Academic Press publications
visit our website at http://store.elsevier.com/

Working together
to grow libraries in
developing countries

www.elsevier.com • www.bookaid.org

Publisher: Sara Tenney
Acquisitions Editor: Elizabeth Brown
Editorial Project Manager: Joslyn Chaiprasert-Paguio
Production Project Manager: Lisa Jones
Designer: Maria Ines Cruz

Typeset by TNQ Books and Journals
www.tnq.co.in

Contents

Preface

Over a 36-year span, I was employed in law enforcement, having served as a patrol officer, detective, crime scene investigator, and photographer. For 25 of those years, I also worked as a latent fingerprint examiner, finally retiring in 2010 from the Florida Department of Law Enforcement as a senior crime laboratory analyst, assigned to the latent print section.

When I attended the basic police academy in 1975, we were taught almost nothing about evidence collection or fingerprint development and preservation. Over the years, things haven't changed much; my son attended the basic police academy five years ago and received about the same amount of training concerning fingerprints. This is partly due to the fact that the instructors were not fingerprint examiners, crime scene personnel, or fully qualified to teach on the subject.

During my career, I had the good fortune to meet many officers from a variety of agencies, including local, state, and federal levels of law enforcement. Invariably, their general knowledge of fingerprint processing and examination was incomplete at best. Most were only familiar with dusting and lifting and thought that identifications were made automatically by computer. Unfortunately, this too seems not to have changed much. Even in those cases where personnel were aware of the existence of additional processes, their knowledge of when and how to apply these processes was limited, and funding for training is scarce.

My intent in compiling this guide is to educate and assist those who process crime scenes and collect and process evidence. In addition, first responders need to know the potential value of evidentiary items located at the crime scene; too often, important pieces are not collected because first responders are not aware that they can be processed.

Many of those responsible for processing fingerprint evidence are not aware that multiple processes can be used on the same piece of evidence if used in the proper sequence. Having taught latent fingerprint development as an adjunct professor, I could not locate a text suitable to use in a fingerprint development course. I hope that this text may fill the void.

Acknowledgments

During my 36-year employment in law enforcement, many people have had an influence on my career. Of these, none were greater than the support of my family. Working as a police officer, I was not always able to lend support to my wife and encouragement to my children at various events because of my work schedule. I missed little league games, birthday parties, and holiday dinners, shortchanging my children and placing additional burdens on my wife. I would like to thank my wife Diane, my daughter Katie, and my son Steve for their understanding.

In addition, I would like to thank the late Michael J. Rafferty, former Chief of Forensics at the Fort Myers Regional Operations Center of the Florida Department of Law Enforcement, for encouraging me to submit various articles for publishing. He was instrumental in my joining the faculty at Edison College as an adjunct professor and becoming a member of the Crime Scene Technology Advisory Committee there. He appointed me to the Quality Assurance Committee–Fingerprint Discipline and to the committee to revise the Latent Print Analysis Training Program and Latent Fingerprint Procedures Manual. It was his advocating that cultivated my decision to write this book.

Chapter 1

The Forensic Science of Fingerprints

Chapter Outline

FINGERPRINTS

Fingerprints are the most dynamic form of evidence in existence… They are unique, permanent, objective and exact… The results are absolute and final.

Fingerprints can be identified to the exclusion of all others, which is not possible by other forms of forensic testing. Even DNA is not as exact, where identical twins have the same DNA.

Robert Hazen, Director of the FBI Latent Fingerprint Section, 1986

The "Science of Fingerprint Identification" begins at the point where material known as a matrix is transferred from an area of friction ridge skin to an object or surface. The "Science" continues on to detection, development, and recovery of the latent print, then to comparison with existing exemplars. The comparison process proceeds until a match or no match conclusion is reached and, ideally, culminates in individualization.

BRIEF HISTORY

For over 2000 years, humankind has known the value of fingerprints as a form of personalization. Chinese craftsmen during the "Tang" Dynasty signed their work with a thumb impression.

Early scientific notices of friction ridge peculiarities include the following:

Dr Nehemiah Grew was the first European to publish friction ridge skin observations. Dutch anatomist Govard Bidloo's 1685 book, "Anatomy of the Human Body," also described friction ridge skin (papillary ridge) details.

Latent Print Processing Guide. http://dx.doi.org/10.1016/B978-0-12-803507-8.00001-8

Marcello Malpighi noted fingerprint ridges, spirals, and loops in his treatise. John Evangelist Purkinje published his thesis discussing nine fingerprint patterns.

No mention of friction ridge skin uniqueness, permanence, or the value of fingerprints for personal identification was made by Grew, Bidloo, Malpighi, or Purkinje.

The first recorded reference to the modern use of fingerprints as a means of identification appeared in 1788 when J.C.A. Mayer wrote, "Although the arrangement of skin ridges is never duplicated in two persons, never the less the similarities are clearer among some individuals. In others the differences are marked, yet in spite of their peculiarities of arrangement all have certain likeness."

The actual use of fingerprints as a means of identification can be traced to India, where in 1858, Sir William James Herschel, a British official in India, began requiring a thumbprint of his subjects when they received goods and supplies. Although initially used as a ruse to prevent fraudulent double-dipping, he noticed that even though fingerprint patterns were similar, a close examination revealed minute differences allowing for individualization.

Other significant dates concerning the evolution of fingerprint identification:

- 1880—Dr Henry Faulds—devised methods for the taking of inked fingerprints that are still in use today.
- 1892—Sir Francis Galton—defined the five ridge detail types, now referred to as the Galton details.
- 1892—Juan Vucetich—the first recorded use of fingerprints for criminal identification (Argentina).
- 1901—Sir Edward Richard Henry—developed the Henry System of classification, a very intricate method for filing fingerprints so they may be located by means other than a subject's name.
- 1904—Fingerprints are officially introduced in the United States at the World's Fair in Saint Louis.
- 1911—Jennings versus Illinois—the first time fingerprints are allowed to be admitted as evidence in the US.
- 1924—The FBI Identification Division was formed.

DEFINITIONS

- *Friction Ridge Skin*—the portion of skin containing peaks and valleys, arranged in a pattern and located on the palmer and plantar surfaces.
- *Palmer Surface*—the palm side of hands, including fingers.
- *Plantar Surface*—the bottom of feet and toes.
- *Latent Fingerprint*—the word latent means to lie hidden or to escape notice. As it refers to crime scenes, latents are fingerprints that are involuntary

recordings of the friction ridge skin scarcely or not visible, but they can be developed for study.

- *Inked Fingerprint*—an inked fingerprint is produced when a thin film of black printer ink is applied to the tops of the ridges present on the last finger joint, after which the finger is pressed against a white card or piece of paper. This effect creates a "stamp" of the fingerprint pattern.
- *Core*—a core is present in the *Loop* and *Whorl* patterns. It is essentially the center of the fingerprint pattern. It can be identified by the innermost recurving ridge in the Loop pattern and the center of the circular pattern in the Whorl.
- *Delta*—deltas are also present in *Loop* and *Whorl* patterns and are formed between the type lines (ridges) that flow in on one side and out on the other at the bottom and the ridges that recurve to encompass the center of the pattern. Their shape is similar to a river delta.

Fingerprint Patterns—fingerprint patterns, or ridge formations, are grouped in three categories, which are then broken down into eight subcategories: Arch, Tented arch, Right and Left slanted Loop, Whorl, Central pocket whorl, Double loop whorl, and Accidental whorl.

The **three basic** pattern forms are the following:

Arch—an Arch pattern is identified by the ridges flowing *in on one side*, forming a gentle "arch," and flowing *out on the other side*.

Loop—the Loop can be distinguished by the formation of a ridge "loop" when at least one ridge flows *in from one side*, recurves, and *exits out the same side* it entered. The Loop also must have one delta.

Whorl—the Whorl is very distinct, as the ridges flow or tend to flow in a *circular pattern*. A whorl pattern contains two deltas.

TYPES OF FINGERPRINTS

The million dollar question... What types of surfaces can you get fingerprints off of?

The answer is pretty much everything: hard surfaces, soft surfaces, porous surfaces (paper), cloth, rock, even human skin. The key here is that a fingerprint is an imprint (reproduction) of a finger or a portion of friction ridge skin and is produced by the *transference* of whatever was present on the surface of that finger or portion of friction ridge skin. This could be anything from perspiration to paint to body oils or food residue. The length of time that a fingerprint will remain is dependent on the makeup of the transferred material.

Fingerprints fall into different categories:

- Latent fingerprints (hidden).
- Patent fingerprints (visible).
- Plastic fingerprints (3D).
- Often these are all referred to as "latents."

WHY FINGERPRINTS ARE USED FOR IDENTIFICATION

- Friction ridge skin on the palmer and plantar surfaces of the hands and feet are **unique** to an individual person.
- The fingerprint patterns and ridge details are **permanent**. Developing in the womb at about the 12th week after conception, fingerprints do not naturally change, except in size, during the life of an individual.

HOW FINGERPRINTS ARE PRODUCED

- **Transfer of contaminants (Matrix)**—this is the primary process that produces a fingerprint on a piece of evidence. Normally, a fingertip will contain little more than a small amount of perspiration. This particular perspiration does not contain oils. The fingers coming in contact with various objects or surfaces pick up other forms of contaminants. When an object is touched, some of the contaminants will transfer to the object, leaving a "print" of the fingers.

  Examples of Matrix:

  Body oils found in the hairy areas (from sebaceous glands)

  Perspiration (eccrine glands on palmer and plantar surfaces)

  Grease

  Blood

  Paint
- **Plastic deformation**—the fingers will often leave an impression in a soft material, such as tacky paint or drying blood, soil, and candle wax (etc.).
- **Material removal**—additionally, fingers coming in contact with a dirty or dusty surface may remove that material, resulting in a clean fingerprint surrounded by the dirt or dust.

DETECTION AND DEVELOPMENT

- First and foremost in the process of fingerprint identification for the purposes of solving crimes is the detection and development of a latent fingerprint of sufficient quality to affect a fingerprint comparison. Second to this is the taking of good quality inked fingerprints for this latent to be compared to.
- Different surfaces and materials require different process techniques in order to develop that "hidden" fingerprint. Basically, there are two types of surfaces, **nonporous** (nonabsorbent) like glass, metal, or plastic and **porous** (absorbent) like paper.

  Like the composition of the matrix, the substrate can also be hard to group into a specific category. The basic categories, nonporous or porous, can actually be a widespread combination of the two. An example of this would be paper. The first reaction might be to place paper into the porous category, but paper can range in density from tissue to high-gloss magazine covers and, as such, must be processed differently.

- **Nonporous** surfaces are usually identified with the more commonly known dusting process using fine powders and a fingerprint brush, followed by applying transparent tape over the developed fingerprint and lifting it. These surfaces can also be treated by exposing the subject item to super glue fumes, which polymerize (adhere) to the latent fingerprint. Subsequently, these cyanoacrylate-treated prints can by powdered and lifted or treated with chemical dye stains, which results with them fluorescing when observed under a particular color of light supplied by an alternate light source.
- **Porous** surfaces usually require the use of a chemical reagent to develop fingerprints so that we may recover and compare them. Chemical reagents react with the contaminant, which has been transferred from the fingertip to the object. This reaction can take two forms: it either makes the latent fingerprint visible under normal lighting conditions or causes the fingerprint to fluoresce under the illumination of the alternate light source. The recovery of these fingerprints requires that they be photographed.

RECOVERY AND PRESERVATION

- The use of **photography**—it is wise to photograph all latents as they are located or developed, as additional recovery processes may alter or destroy the previously developed latent, rendering it useless. In some cases, as with forensic light source detection, iodine fuming, and silver nitrate, the results are not permanent and must be photographed, or they will eventually be lost. Photography is a permanent record, which can be reproduced many times and can be enhanced by using different types of development (dark room) techniques and software. When photographing latents, include an item in the frame, such as a coin or preferably a small stick-on scale, so that the photo can be reproduced life size when printing.
- **Lifting**—latents developed with powder can be preserved by placing a piece of clear cellophane tape over the dusted latent, causing the dust to adhere to the adhesive side of the tape. This tape is then lifted from the object and placed on a card or backer, which has a contrasting color to the powder used, resulting in a print that is in the same alignment as an inked fingerprint.
- **Casting**—fingerprints left in soft putty, drying paint, or blood can be cast using tool mark recovery methods, such as commercial silicone rubber casting material, which may include, but is not limited to, Duplicast™, Mikrosil™, or Accutrans™ (polyvinylsiloxane).

FINGERPRINT IDENTIFICATION

- To identify a fingerprint is to say that a particular unknown fingerprint matches a second known or unknown fingerprint in all details. Upon identification, the examiner is affirming that two fingerprints have been produced by the same individual.

- An example of the method to complete this process is as follows:
- Identify **class characteristics**—this involves determining the shape, ridge flow, and pattern type of a fingerprint. These are called level 1 details. Being able to determine the class characteristics can immediately eliminate a fingerprint as a possible candidate. Knowing that your subject fingerprint is a particular pattern type can eliminate all other pattern types from consideration. Pattern identification—shape and ridge flow can be a strong indicator of pattern type and even right or left hand or palm. Subtle ridge flow curvature can sometimes be enough to identify the source of the questioned friction ridge.
- Identify **ridge details**—once it has been determined that the class characteristics of two fingerprints are similar, an examination for identical ridge detail is performed. **Ridge or "Galton" details**, level 2 details, are located in one fingerprint. Usually a pair of prominent details is chosen to make the search easier, and the location and ridge spacing is carefully noted. An attempt is then made to locate these details on the second fingerprint. They must be the same in both fingerprints in order to proceed. After concluding they are identical, a third detail is located and compared, then a fourth, and so on. Sometimes level 3 details are present in both the latent and inked fingerprint and can also be used to affect identification. Level 3 details consist of pore detail and individual ridge shape. When the examiner is satisfied that a sufficient quantity of matching detail is present, a positive identification is declared. **No minimum** number of points has been set by US authorities.

AFIS (Automated Fingerprint Identification System)

- A computer system that has the ability to sort through thousands of fingerprint cards and retrieve exemplar, or known, fingerprints that are *similar* to the questioned fingerprint. The system should be more accurately referred to as a computer-aided fingerprint identification system, as AFIS does not automatically identify fingerprints; the identification is done by a latent fingerprint examiner.
- Upon the arrest of an individual, the fingerprints are searched against a database containing the fingerprints of persons previously arrested. Many times people give false information at the time of arrest, and with the AFIS system, these incidents are detected and the arrested party is found to have an arrest warrant or is in violation of their probation.
- Additionally, latent fingerprints are entered into the AFIS system and are searched against the database. The computer generates a list of **possible** candidates and displays the fingerprints associated with that list. This affords us the ability to solve crimes when there is not an initial suspect.

Chapter 2

Developing Fingerprints

Chapter Outline

CHEMICAL AND PHYSICAL PROCESSES

Skin Structure

- Dermis and epidermis—Friction ridge skin is comprised of two main layers: the dermis and epidermis. The epidermis is the exterior or outer layer. The dermis lies under the epidermis next to muscle tissue. Contained in these main layers are several other layers and the **eccrine** glands, which secrete perspiration (see Figure 1).
- Epidermal cells are produced in the basal layer, sometimes called the generating layer, and migrate toward the surface, where they eventually exfoliate (slough off). This generating layer contains the template for the fingerprint pattern and details. A laceration passing through the generating layer will result in the formation of a scar (see Figure 2).
- Horny skin cells are also called epithelial cells and are valuable for DNA examinations.

Chemical Composition of Perspiration

98.5–99.5% water (salt (sodium) is the second largest component)

- Eccrine Glands:
  Palmar and **Plantar** surfaces of hands and feet
  Inorganic:
  - Halides (mainly chloride)
  - Ammonia
  - Sulfate
  - Phosphate
  - ***Sodium**
  - Calcium

  Organic:
  - ***Amino acids**
  - Urea
  - Lactic acid
  - Sugars
  - Creatine
  - Choline
  - Uric acid
  - Riboflavins
  - Pyridoxin
- Sebaceous Glands:
  Hairy body areas
  Organic:
  - ***Fatty acids**
  - Glycerides

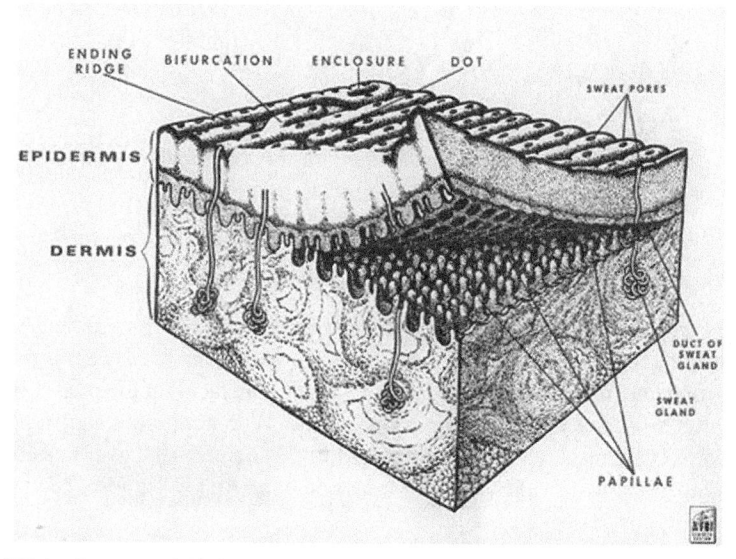

FIGURE 1 Structure of friction skin. *Federal Bureau of Investigation, 1990. The Science of Fingerprints. US Department of Justice.*

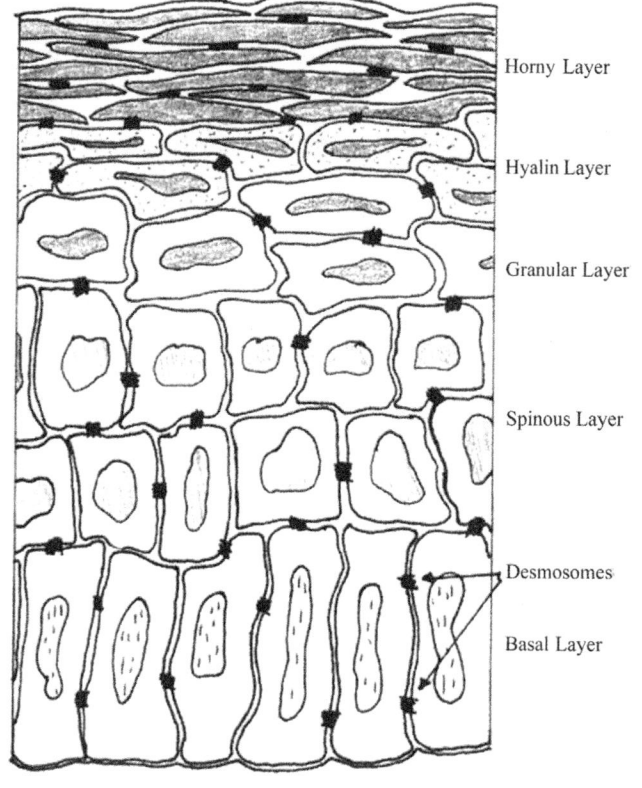

Horny Layer

Hyalin Layer

Granular Layer

Spinous Layer

Desmosomes

Basal Layer

FIGURE 2 Skin layers. *Ashbaugh, D.R., 1999. Quantitative–Qualitative Friction Ridge Analysis. CRC Press, Boca Raton, Florida.*

Hydrocarbons
Alcohols

*These, along with proteins and heme, are the chemicals produced by the body that are targeted by reagents in chemical processing.

Chemical Processing versus Physical Processing

The first consideration when choosing chemical or physical processing is the type of surface or substrate you are going to process. In most cases, porous items will be chemically processed, mainly due to the fact that the matrix of the latent print will have absorbed into the substrate. With nonporous items, physical processes are used, either going straight to powder or, whenever possible, it is recommended that cyanoacrylate fuming be done first to stabilize the latent, followed by powder or dye staining.

In Chapter 4, Protocols and Methods, processing techniques and their order of application are laid out for a variety of surfaces. These should be adaptable to any substrate situation you might encounter. The application sequence is extremely critical because some processes preclude the use of additional processes, limiting the development of evidence.

- A good rule of thumb in determining porous from nonporous surfaces is to imagine placing a couple of drops of water on the surface; if you think the water would run off, it is nonporous.
  Some surfaces are also considered semiporous and, when processed sequentially, can be treated as both.
- Chemical processes *transform the composition* of the original fingerprint.
  Chemical processes are normally limited to use on porous surfaces (except dye stains), but a few, like iodine and RTX, can be used on either porous or nonporous surfaces.
- Physical processes *enhance the appearance* of the fingerprint.
- Chemical processing is identified by whether or not the resultant fingerprint has been altered rather than just added to (such as powder). A chemical that might be considered in this group is iodine. However, since the effects of iodine fuming eventually wear off, it is a physical process, as is powder and Cyanoacrylate fuming.

Preprocessing Measures

Prior to jumping into slinging powder and spraying chemicals, a few administrative measures need to be addressed and processes triaged before moving forward to assure that your efforts are not wasted. Court provisions must be met and a logical sequence of process application be laid out to maximize results and ensure those results are accepted as evidence.

Chain of Custody/Chain of Evidence

Handling evidence requires an unbroken chain of custody in order for it to be offered for court presentation. Proper documentation should be maintained as to the location where the evidence was found, the date it was located, who found it, and who collected it. The exterior packaging should be sealed with evidence tape and signed or initialed across the seal. When the packaging is opened for processing, the original seal should not be broken; instead, the package should be opened in a different place, so the new location can be sealed, dated, and initialed. If for any reason the original packaging can no longer be used, repack the evidence and include the original packaging with the evidence in the new package. This will maintain the chain of custody by showing each instance when the evidence package was opened and resealed.

It is also necessary to maintain a log indicating transfers between analysts and also between the analysts and the evidence custodian.

Evidence Processing Strategies

As stated previously, with the variety of processes available for both porous and nonporous surfaces (plus all surfaces in between), planning the order of application of these processes should be your first step. Considerations such as the stability and durability of the surface, whether it would stand up to particular processes, and whether there are other disciplines that should examine the evidence prior to or in concert with fingerprint processing as my process may preclude other discipline processes. Inspect the evidence for inherent fluorescence; processes that require examination under a forensic light source may also cause the background to fluoresce and eliminate the contrast you are trying to create. Preplanning your sequence of process applications will assure the best possibility for positive results.

Documentation of Original Appearance

Processing evidence for the presence of fingerprints can alter its appearance, causing changes in color, causing certain inks to run, or damaging the surface of some substrates. Documentation of printed material, in particular handwritten notes or signed checks and documents, should be done either by photography or photocopy. Items may be submitted for handwriting analysis as well as fingerprint development and a determination as to which would be done first should be made. Sometimes a handwriting analysis can be done from copies or photos.

Avoiding Cross-contamination

Often the crime scene will be coated with blood and or body fluids. An attempt should be made to prevent cross-contamination where DNA evidence may be present. Careful handling of body fluids also lessens the risk of biohazard infection to the analyst. The forensic supply retailers are now marketing single-use fingerprint brushes and powder containers, as well as other products to help with these concerns.

Documentation of Process Application

It may be prudent to keep a log of when a process occurred, what process occurred, and what the result of the process was.

Example:

12/12/12 Processed with Ninhydrin results—three latents of value, sent to photography

12/16/12 Processed with physical developer—no additional latents developed

This may come up in court during cross-examination. Word of mouth does not carry as much weight in courtroom testimony.

Whenever possible, the evidence should be marked with the initials of the analyst. Indelible ink, a china marker (grease pencil), or a scribe should be used so that the markings withstand processing.

Visual Examination

As you will see in Chapter 4, visual examination is listed first in the protocol sequences for all the substrate types. I compare fingerprint development to suspect interrogation; during interrogation, the interviewer has to coax the suspect to talk but also faces the possibility that if he is too aggressive, the suspect may invoke their Miranda rights. Fingerprint development is similar in that being too aggressive can result in losing valuable evidence. Visual examination is nondestructive, allowing for additional examination without the possibility for damaging fragile latents. Certain latents may not respond to processing techniques. An example would be latents on a dusty surface, where the matrix is not transferred, but instead the dust is transferred to the fingertip. In this instance, powder processing may remove the rest of the dust, and with no lipids or other contaminants present, powdering or cyanoacrylate fuming would not be effective. By exposing the evidence to an oblique light source and adjusting the angle of incidence, differences in the reflectance between the dusty and clean areas will be made visible. This allows the analyst to recover the visualized latent by photography. An exercise to illustrate this result would involve placing a fingerprint on the flat side of the shiny blade of a butter knife; by rotating or twisting it, you will observe the print change from visible to invisible.

A visual examination is also recommended using a forensic light source, at least in the 450 nm (blue light) range, to determine if the substrate or matrix has inherent fluorescence.

It is imperative that any results from visual examination or any other processes be photographed prior to moving on to the next processes because what you have may be all you get. Even though the process sequences are designed to limit the loss of latents, it is possible that the next process in the sequence may have that result.

CHEMICAL PROCESSING

Chemical Process Types

There are basically two types of chemical processes used in fingerprint development:

- **Reagents**
- **Dye stain**

  Note: the second, dye stain, is truly a physical process because it only enhances the appearance of the latent print, but it is generally grouped with chemical processes because of the application method.

Reagents

- **Reagents, as applied to fingerprint development, are *reactive* with a number of body fluid components**. First are **lipids or sebum**, second are **amino acids**, third are **sodium or salt**, and the latter two are present primarily in perspiration from eccrine glands. Other reagents are reactive with **protein and hemoglobin** present in **blood**.

Dye Stain

- Dye stains are used to add visible color or a fluorescent stain to fingerprints previously processed with **Cyanoacrylate** (super glue), allowing existing latent fingerprints to be seen either with the naked eye or through the use of a **forensic light source**.
  It should be noted that most reagents and dye stains are solvent based, that is the reagent is mixed with methanol or ethanol (etc.), which can have a harmful reaction with certain materials. Plastics and painted or varnished surfaces can be deteriorated when contacted by some solvents. There are a few processes that have an aqueous formulation as well that will avoid this problem.

Detection and Development

Contaminant

1. **Lipids**—If Iodine fuming is to be used, it must be the first step, as the following procedures will preclude the possibility of going back. (A physical developer is also reported to develop lipid prints but must be used as the last process.)
   Iodine fuming is a nondestructive process. Both lipids, which are produced by the sebaceous glands, and amino acids are almost always present in latent print matrix. Normally the iodine fuming process is skipped in favor of the Ninhydrin or the analog processes because they are more productive. However, if you are dealing with artwork or historical documents, the nondestructive iodine process would be preferable because there are no lasting effects, and the developed print dissipates after a short time.

2. **Amino acid**—This is the organic component most targeted by chemical processing. There are several reagent choices available, and these, in turn, have application protocols.

    Amino Acid Reagents:

    - DFO—Diazafluoren-9-one—a fluorescing reagent
    - IND—1,2-Indanedione—also a fluorescing reagent

      Note: DFO and IND must be applied prior to Ninhydrin, as it will interfere with the fluorescent properties of DFO and IND.

    - NIN—Ninhydrin—Visualization can take up to 24h without heat acceleration (Ruhemann's purple color). This is the last applied amino acid reagent.

    After processing, NIN residue remains on the entire document and will still react with amino acid. It is imperative that while handling the documents postprocessing, that no contact be made without latex gloves being worn. Inadvertent touching of the document will most probably result in the development of the analysts' fingerprints on the evidence in approximately 24h or less, which might complicate prosecution.

3. **Sodium chloride**—Silver nitrate is used to detect the presence of latent fingerprints containing salt deposits. Physical developer contains silver nitrate and is thought to also develop sodium latents.

4. **Proteins and Heme**—These are contained in fingerprints contaminated with blood. Various processes are available to develop blood prints and will be discussed later. If it is known or suspected that blood prints may be present, it is recommended that the blood processes be applied first.

Reagent Application

- The use of liquid reagents and dye stains requires that certain safety steps be taken. Wherever possible, these liquids should be applied in a chemical fume hood (see Figure 3).
- The spray method is considered the most hazardous, as very fine particles are launched into the immediate area of the analyst and may cause them to become contaminated. Use of a respirator is recommended if the spray method is employed and no fume hood is available. The handheld pump sprayer (see Figure 4) is the most common device used for spraying and is beneficial by allowing the analyst to control the amount of developer/dye stain being applied. At times the substrate being processed can be damaged by overwetting (such as kleenex or tissue paper).
- A second method, dipping, is preferred based on safety. In this method, the item is simply immersed in the developer/dye stain, removed, and allowed to dry. Depending on the process, this method is sometimes required due to a minimum time of exposure to the liquid (i.e., dip item for "*" seconds). Use of varying sizes of glass bakeware is recommended for containing the developer/dye stain as they are readily available and can be easily cleaned (see Figure 5).

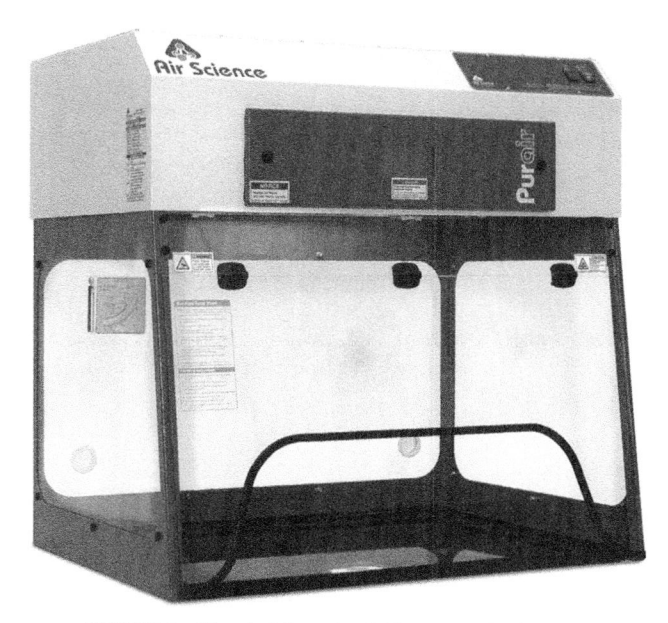

FIGURE 3 Chemical fume hood. *Courtesy of Air Science.*

FIGURE 4 Hand pump sprayer. *Courtesy of Arrowhead Forensics.*

FIGURE 5   Glass Bakeware.

FIGURE 6   Chemical wash bottle. *Courtesy of Arrowhead Forensics.*

- Another method is an extension of the dip method and is referred to as the wash method. At times the item being processed is too large to be dipped, and by means of the wash method, the developer/dye stain is simply poured or washed over the surface. Typically, a chemical wash bottle is used, helping to control the amount of liquid used (see Figure 6).
- Since different reagents react with distinct components of body fluids, more than one reagent can be used on the same piece of evidence. Through years of testing, it has been determined that the application of these reagents must follow a set *protocol*.

Reagent Development

Whether spraying, dipping, or using the wash bottle, the porous items should be completely wet so as to take on a translucent appearance. They then should be allowed to dry completely.

After application, certain reagents require "development" by either heating, as in the case of DFO, IND, and NIN, or exposing to a strong white light source for silver nitrate.

The heat source can be provided by laboratory oven, simple steam iron, heat and humidity chamber, or photo mounting press. Passing a steam iron over processed paper will develop the NIN prints but may also cause the paper to curl, and caution should be taken not to get any condensation on the document. When using a photo mounting press, place the documents in a protective "envelope" made from folded brown wrapping (craft) paper and position the packet between the platens.

Chemical Process Types

Typical process **sequence for porous items**:

1. Visual
2. Iodine fume to detect **oils** (lipids)
3. DFO or IND to detect **amino acids** (fluorescent process requires examination using an alternate light source in the 450 nm range)
4. Ninhydrin to detect **amino acids**
5. Silver nitrate to detect **salts** (sodium)
6. Physical developer to detect **lipids** or **salts**

Personal Protective Equipment (PPE)

PPE should be employed while processing with chemicals (including cyanoacrylate fuming) or fingerprint powders; they can include, but are not limited to, the following:

- Vinyl or nitrile gloves
- Particle face masks or respirators
- Eye protection
- Sturdy closed-toe shoes
- Lab coat or apron

Mixing Supplies

A number of the processes are available commercially but many are not. Some of the chemicals listed in the formulas are only available from chemical companies like Sigma–Aldrich, Fisher Scientific, and Alfa (etc.). Mixing the chemistry requires some specialized equipment; the following is a list of those that are the most helpful:

An accurate balance
Weigh boats

Graduated cylinders
Beakers (a variety of sizes up to one gal)
Pipettes
Magnetic stirrer
Glass or fiberglass stirring rods
Storage containers (some amber colored)
Glass liquid separator
Filter paper
Orbital shaker

PHYSICAL PROCESSING

Development with Powders

When to Use Powders

- The decision to process an item with fingerprint powder starts with the type of substrate that the latent is believed to be located on. Most often we are looking at nonporous items such as glass, metal, or plastic. Some paper products are also candidates for powder processing if the finish on the paper is glossy.
- A good rule of thumb in determining porous from nonporous surfaces is to imagine placing a couple of drops of water on the surface; if you think the water would run off, it is a nonporous surface.
- Some surfaces are also considered semiporous and, when processed sequentially, can be treated as both.

Equipment

- The equipment list for powder processing is short, but choosing the right equipment is sometimes tricky:
- Powder type and color (fluorescent required?)
- Brush type
- Recovery material or method

Powder Selection

- The type and color of powder used to develop a latent print is dependent on several factors:
- Background color
- Choose a *contrasting color* (see Figure 7)
- Choose a *fluorescent powder for multicolored backgrounds* (see Figure 8)
  Note: before applying fluorescent powder, observe the evidence under UV light. If the evidence fluoresces, this might preclude the use of fluorescent powder or determine the color of fluorescent powder used. Using black powder and photo shop is another alternative.
- Type of substrate
- Personal preference

FIGURE 7   Gray, black, and white powders.

FIGURE 8   Green and pink fluorescent powders.

Brush Selection

- Normal powders are applied using a fiberglass filament brush or a camel hair or squirrel hair brush. Fiberglass seems to be the brush of choice, using the camel or squirrel hair to "clean out" an overpowdered print.
- Feather brushes are normally reserved for fluorescent powders but can also be used for normal powders (see Figure 9).
- The last brush type is not a brush at all; rather, it is a small magnet at the end of a wand. This is for the application of magnetic powders (see Figure 10).
- Cross-contamination of powder colors should be avoided. One fiberglass brush should be dedicated for black powder and one for white. The same holds true for fluorescent powder (one red, one green).

FIGURE 9 Nylon filament brush, camel hair brush, and feather brush.

FIGURE 10 Gray magnetic powder and applicators.

- The nylon filament brush handle is twirled between the thumb and forefinger so that the filament spreads like a helicopter. The other brushes are used in the standard manner. The camel hair brush is handy when too much powder has been applied. Brushing lightly in the direction of the ridge flow will remove excess powder.

Method

- A small amount of powder is applied to the brush by dipping the brush into the container gently and then shaking off the excess.
- The brush is then gently brought into contact with the object of evidence and the powder spread in what I call a "scouting" procedure.
- This "scouting" process will start to expose latents without overpowdering. Gray or silver powders have a tendency to clump, so use sparingly.
- Once latents are observed, the powdering is continued in a motion that follows the flow of the ridges—not across, as that may rub off the latent. This is repeated until a print of sufficient density (darkness) is developed.

Note: a UV or black light is required when using fluorescent powders. When applying fluorescent powders, it is very easy to end up using too much. This results in strong background fluorescence as well as the developed fingerprint. A tip is to pour about ¼ inch of the powder into a small paper cup and then pour it back into the container; the powder remaining in the cup will be enough.

Recovery and Preservation

- The recovery of powdered prints from nonporous surfaces involves the use of transparent tape and backer cards (see Figure 11), which contrast the color of the powder. The tape is arched so that the center contacts the developed latent print first, and then the tape is smoothed outward toward the edges. This reduces the chance that air bubbles will form. This procedure is repeated when placing the lifting material on the backer card (see Figures 12–14).

For chain of custody purposes, record the location from where the lift was taken, the date, and the case number and initial the back of the lift card.

The Second Lift

In some cases, an overabundance of powder will cling to contamination surrounding the latent, nearly obliterating it. Lifting this contaminated latent will remove the surrounding contamination. Lightly repowdering the area, then taking a second lift will result in a much cleaner, clearer print. Label the lifts #1 and #2.

There are many different sizes of lifting tapes and also a variety of tape materials. Some tapes are flexible and are more suited for irregular and textured surfaces.

The hinged lifters (see Figure 15) come in various sizes with the lifting tape and the backer attached. A cellophane protector must be removed from the adhesive side and then the fingerprint lifted normally. Finally, the adhesive side of the tape

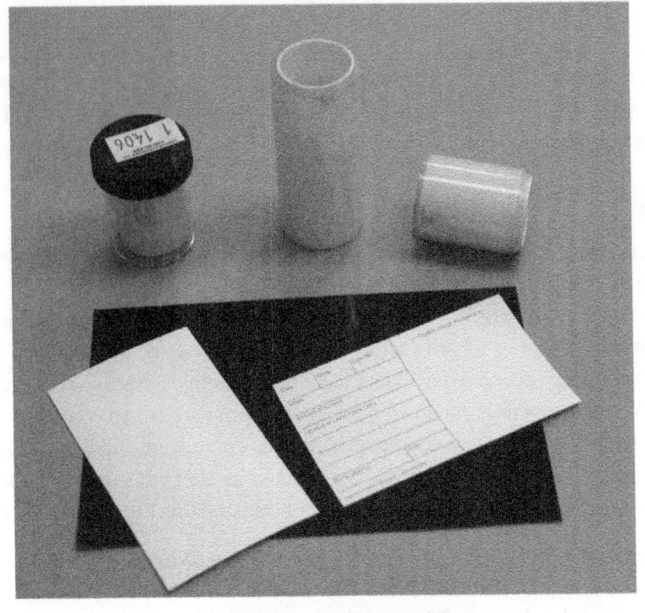

FIGURE 11 Lifting materials.

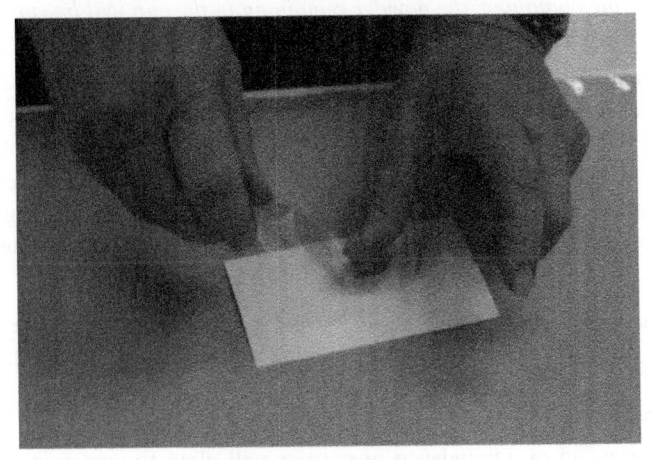

FIGURE 12 Arching the tape.

is folded over the backer. One advantage of the hinged lifter is that the attached backer acts like a handle while trying to place the lifter over the fingerprint.

The rubber lifters (see Figure 16) are very flexible and can be used on irregular shaped items. They are opaque, so the resulting lift will be in reverse orientation. The adhesive is on what would be the backer card on other types of lifts and is then covered with clear plastic protector.

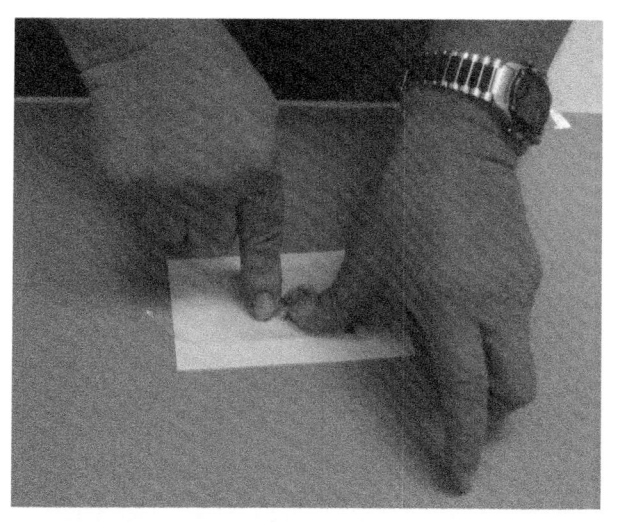

FIGURE 13   Press in the center and smooth outward.

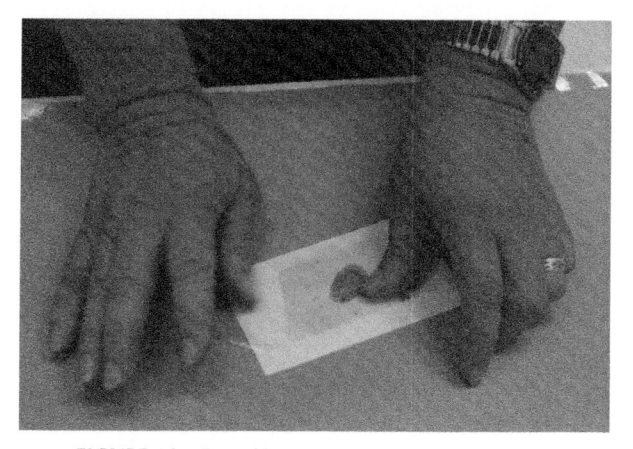

FIGURE 14   Smoothing outward to prevent air bubbles.

Lifting Palm Prints

When recovering a developed palm print, it is necessary to record the entire print on a single lift. This is important because the fingerprint examiner is allowed to use "points" from adjacent fingers to affect an identification, as long as they can demonstrate that those fingers came from the same hand and were placed there at the same time.

This can be accomplished by using a large hinged lifter or when using tape. Place tape strips side by side, slightly overlapping them by approximately one quarter inch, until the entire palm print is covered. Lifting can be cumbersome,

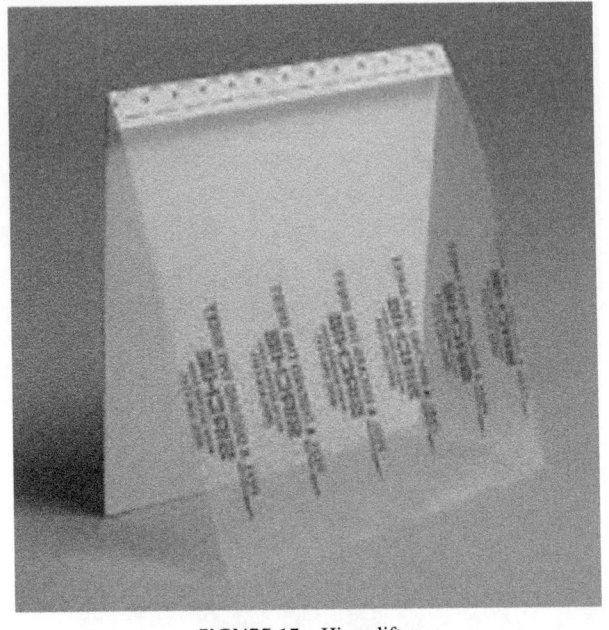

FIGURE 15 Hinge lifter.

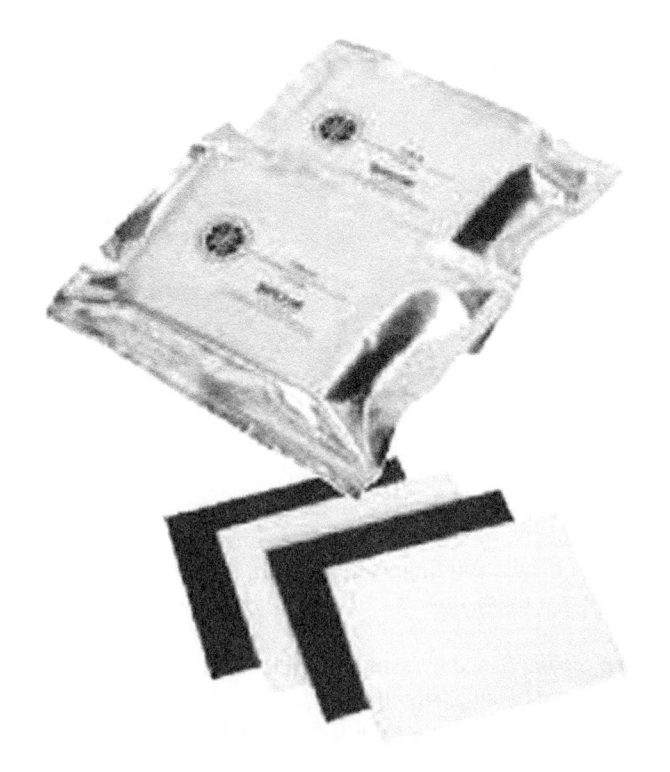

FIGURE 16 Rubber gel lifters.

but by starting at the first placed strip and lifting carefully, it can be done. Once lifted, place the tape on a backing of contrasting color.

- Photography can also be used to recover latent from irregular surfaces or at any time you feel it more prudent than an attempt to lift the print. Remember you sometimes only have one shot at the lift.
- For porous and semiporous surfaces you have powder processed, photography is used to recover latent from surfaces you feel will be damaged while attempting to lift the print. It is best to photograph the print and cover it with tape to preserve it.

Powder Ingredients

Black powder will contain some of the following:

- Carbon black
- Lycopodium
- Black oxide
- Gum arabic

White powder will contain some of the following:

- Alumina hydrate
- Silica, amorphous
- Titanium dioxide
- Zinc stearate
- Aluminum
- Stearic acid

Fluorescent Powder will contain some of the following:

- Zinc sulfide
- Rocket red AX pigment
- All magnetic powders will contain iron in combination with the other ingredients.

Small Particle Reagent (SPR)

- Powder suspended in a mixture of Photo-flo and water
- Five grams of Molybdenum Disulfide powder is mixed with 0.4 ml Photo-flo or Liqua-nox (detergent) and 50 ml distilled water.
- Primarily used on items that are wet or were previously wet
- The mixture is placed in a spray bottle and is sprayed onto the evidence being processed while continually agitating the mixture to keep the powder in suspension.

The result is a light gray fingerprint that can be photographed or lifted after it has dried.

Sticky Side Powder

Put fingerprint powder on the adhesive side of tape? Yes, a method very similar to SPR (small particle reagent) is used on the sticky side of tape. It is a slurry of powder and Photo-flo combined to the consistency of thick paint. The mixture is painted on the adhesive with a camel hair brush, allowed to dry for a couple of minutes, and then rinsed under running water.

Nonporous Process Protocol/Sequence

- A typical process **sequence for nonporous items**:
  1. Visual
  2. Cyanoacrylate (super glue) whenever possible
  3. Dye stain after cyanoacrylate
  4. Observe under forensic light source
  5. Powder
  6. Other physical processes include visual, **casting**, and **alternate light source**

Iodine fuming, although a chemical, is also a physical process, as it does not change the chemical composition of the fingerprint. It is nondestructive, and if it is used first, it does not preclude the use of further processing (i.e., steps 2–6).

CYANOACRYLATE PROCESSING

Principle

- Used primarily on nonporous surfaces
- As cyanoacrylate cures or hardens, vapors are released into the surrounding atmosphere. As these vapors contact articles in close proximity, they polymerize to various contaminants present on those items. In doing so, a white residue becomes visible.
- Fingerprints are a prime source of the contaminants which attract Cyanoacrylate (CA) vapors.

Definitions

- *CA*—Cyanoacrylate monomer, super glue
- *Polymerization*—A chemical reaction causing molecules of CA to rapidly bond to one another. Polymerization retardants are added to CA to slow this reaction. Under magnification, it is possible to see how the CA forms microscopic "chains" as the molecules attach to one another.
- *Vapors*—As CA cures or "hardens" nonpolymerized CA, is carried in vapor form to the object. These vapors are free of retardants.
- *Chemical acceleration*—A heat generating process caused by a chemical reaction (exothermic).

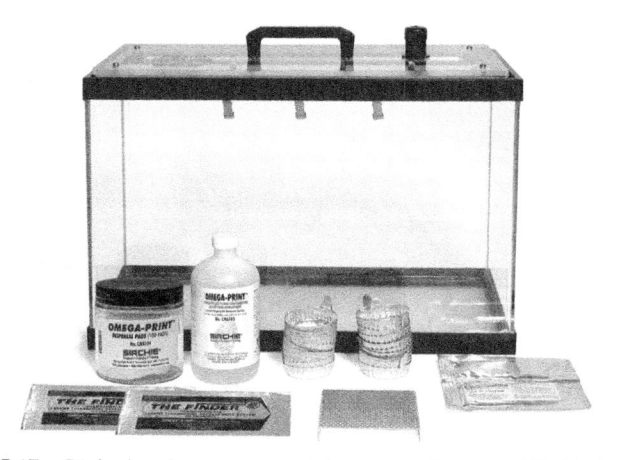

FIGURE 17   CA fuming chamber—converted aquarium. *Courtesy of Sirchie Products.*

- *Vacuum chamber*—Vacuum process for CA
- *Dye Stain*—Fluorescent chemical that attaches to CA molecules.

Contaminants

- CA vapors generally polymerize to the following:
  Lipids
  Heat source
  Moisture
  Organic contaminants
  Cured CA (polymerized)

CA Process

- When items are suspected of containing latent fingerprints, they are placed in a covered semiairtight (closed) container and suspended over a small amount of CA, which is placed in an open container such as a disposable weigh boat. These containers or chambers can range from aquariums (see Figure 17) to custom-built cabinets and can be converted refrigerators or a cardboard box placed inside a trash bag.
- A slight increase in humidity is desired, so an open container of warm water can also be placed in the chamber with the CA and evidence.
- At ambient temperatures, the development process takes approximately three to four hours for latents of sufficient density to appear.
- The addition of heat to the CA speeds up the vaporization stage. Placing the container of CA on a small coffee cup warmer (see Figure 18) in the chamber will reduce the process time to 20–30 min.
- Overdevelopment can easily occur during the CA process if the evidence is exposed to the vapors for too long. One way to prevent this is to place an

FIGURE 18 Cup warmer. *Courtesy of Arrowhead Forensics.*

amount of CA in the chamber that will exhaust its production of vapor at the same time the development process is complete. A rule of thumb is one drop of CA to one gallon (aquarium) of chamber size (i.e., 10 gallon aquarium = 10 drops of CA). When observation of the process is possible, including a test strip with a control fingerprint placed on it will also allow the analyst to detect the proper development time. If proper development is observed and fumes still continue from the CA source, it is necessary to vent the chamber, if it can be done safely, or remove the evidence from the chamber, again being cautious of the CA fumes. Eliminate any heat source if one is being used.

- Note: caution should be taken to avoid contact with CA vapors. They are sweet-smelling, but if directly inhaled, an effect like a slap in the face will occur. Analysts wearing corrective eyewear have also reported a film being produced on their glasses.

Chemical Accelerants

- Sodium hydroxide pad:
  20 grams of sodium hydroxide is dissolved in one liter of distilled water. Cotton batten is cut into two-inch squares and then soaked in the solution and allowed to dry. To use, the pads are placed on a small plate or weigh boat and soaked with cyanoacrylate. This creates vapors rapidly; the fuming process is complete in less than five minutes.
- Mixing baking soda and sawdust (cellulose) together (one to two teaspoons) also causes an accelerated reaction time, although it is slower than sodium hydroxide pads.

Applying the CA to the above pads or mixtures causes an exothermic reaction. This is useful in the field when no electricity is available. *It should be noted that as much as two-thirds of the CA will be used to create the exothermic reaction, leaving only a third to develop latents.*

Cyan O Wand/Fume-A-Wand™

The Cyan O Wand or Fume-A-Wand (see Figure 19) is a handheld, butane-fueled cyanoacrylate fuming device that can be taken to the crime scene and

FIGURE 19   Fume-A-Wand. *Courtesy of Arrowhead Forensics.*

used directly on items that cannot be returned to the lab for processing. A small butane torch heats a cartridge impregnated with CA, generating the CA fumes. This device should be used where adequate ventilation is present. Overdevelopment can occur quickly, so it is necessary to monitor the process closely.

Dye Stains

Dye stains are applied to the cyanoacrylate-developed fingerprints to make them visible under various wavelengths of light. This light energy is supplied by various apparatuses, referred to as forensic light sources or alternate light sources (FLS or ALS). Most of the dye stain formulae are solvent based. When used on varnished and some painted surfaces, the solvent will permeate these surfaces, resulting in the background fluorescing as well as the fingerprint. There is one dye stain process that is water based, Rhodamine 6G aqueous, that will not permeate the finish.

Dye Stain Application

CA processed items should be allowed to "rest" for 15–20 min after being removed from the fuming chamber prior to any further processing. Dye stains can be applied by the spray, wash, or dip method. After being applied evenly, making sure all surfaces are coated and after drying, the items are examined under the prescribed wavelength of light by observing them through the appropriate blocking filter. Some dye stains require that the items be rinsed in water and allowed to dry prior to alternate light source examination.

Note: before applying dye stains, observe the evidence under the appropriate light wavelength (see the following chart). If the evidence fluoresces, this might preclude the use of dye stain or require the use of a dye stain that fluoresces at a different wavelength.

Dye Stain (Partial List)	FLS Light Wavelength (Nanometers)
• Ardrox	300–450 nm
• Basic red	450 nm
• Basic yellow	300–450 nm
• MBD (7-P methoxybenzylamino- 4-nitrobenz-2 oxa-1-3-diazole)	450 nm
• M-star	450 nm
• Rhodamine 6G (mild carcinogen)	450–480 nm
• R.A.M. (Rhodamine, Ardrox, MBD mixture)	300–480 nm
• Safranin-O	450 nm
• TEC (thenoyl europium chelate)	365 nm long wave UV

Dye stains are applied by dipping, washing, or spraying (in fume hood). Ardrox and M-Star require rinsing in slowly running tap water after application. Dye staining does not preclude the use of powders. CA processed fingerprints can be powdered and lifted numerous times.

Forensic Light Source/Alternate Light Source (FLS/ALS)

The objective of causing the ridge detail to fluoresce is to create contrast between the fingerprint and the background or substrate, making it visible for photography. An ALS examination of the substrate should be done prior to processing to determine if the background color or material is fluorescent and at what incident light wavelength. Obviously if the background fluoresces, there will be no contrast, and the use of another wavelength or dye stain might be required.

The process by which fluorescence is achieved starts with a bright light source: mercury, halogen, LED, or xenon bulbs are the most common. By directing the light through a filter, known as a band pass filter, a light of a specific color or wavelength measured in nanometers is produced. A band pass filter only allows a specified wavelength to pass through, plus or minus a small percentage of error. Next, the item to be tested is exposed to the filtered light (incident light). When fluorescence occurs, *a new wavelength of light is emitted:* this phenomenon is known as Stokes shift (http://en.wikipedia.org/wiki/Stokes_shift). This new emitted light is very weak, compared to the incident light coming from the FLS, and is invisible to the naked eye. At this point, a blocking filter is placed between the incident light and the analysts' view to block the FLS-generated light and allow the emitted light to pass. The result is then recovered by photography using a blocking filter over the lens.

Forensic light sources trace their roots to the late 1970s or early 1980s, when various forensic labs and research agencies were using high-powered lasers to illuminate and excite various materials to fluoresce. Argon ion and copper vapor lasers were two of the early types that produced a beam of collimated light, blue/green from the Argon ion and yellow from the copper vapor. These lasers required a large power source and coolers to dissipate sizable amounts of heat generated by the process; they were also very costly. The laser at the FBI Academy filled one room and was actually quite dangerous. It was later determined that collimated light was not required to achieve fluorescence. Today, FLS or ALS can be anything from lasers to light sources with multiwavelength capabilities to sophisticated LED flashlights.

BLOOD PRINT PROCESSING

- Blood prints and blood spatter are most times present in ample supply at homicide scenes. Processes like luminol help us to see the blood patterns not visible to the naked eye. Luminol, however, cannot be used to develop fingerprints to the extent where the detail is good enough for comparison. Other processes exist that will develop blood for fingerprint comparison.
- When sweeping a crime scene or inspecting evidence using the 450 NM setting on your ALS, blood will absorb the blue light and appear dark or black. Ketchup will mimic blood under the 450 NM setting, but a fluorescent "halo" will circle the stain, which is caused by ingredients that have leached to the edge. In any case, a presumptive test would be in order.

Blood Reagents

- Three types of reagents are available to develop fingerprints left in blood
  - Protein developers
  - Heme developers
  - Amino acid developers

Note: hemoglobin, as it decomposes, separates into heme and protein. That is why more than one processing type is recommended and sometimes necessary.

Protein Developers

- **Amido black**—A dark blue stain that turns the protein in blood to dark blue ridges.
  - Amido black is applied by spraying, dipping, or by wash bottle.
  - After treating with Amido, a rinse is applied to wash away background coloring.
  - Amido is not suitable for porous items, such as cloth, due to its staining nature
- **Coomassie blue**—Also a dark blue stain that turns the protein in blood to dark blue ridges.
  - Coomassie blue is applied by spraying, dipping, or by wash bottle.
  - After treating with Coomassie, a rinse is applied to wash away background coloring.

- Coomassie is also not suitable for porous items, such as cloth, due to its staining nature.
- **Crowle's double stain**—Also a dark blue/black stain that turns the protein in blood to dark blue/black ridges.
  - Crowle's is applied by spraying, dipping, or by wash bottle.
  - After treating with Crowle's, a rinse is applied to wash away background coloring.
  - Crowle's is also not suitable for porous items, such as cloth, due to its staining nature.
  - **Acid Yellow 7**—A fluorescent protein stain used on dark colored, nonporous, and porous surfaces. Acid yellow 7 is applied by spraying, dipping, or by wash bottle. (Requires use of an ALS to visualize.)

Heme Developer

- **Leucocrystal Violet (LCV)**—A relatively colorless reagent that can be mixed or purchased as a kit.
  LCV is applied by spraying, dipping, or by wash bottle.
  After treating with LCV, a rinse not necessary.
  LCV is suitable for porous items, such as cloth; due to its colorless nature, it will not stain the background.
- **Luminol** reacts with heme
- **Phenolphthalein** presumptive test reacts with heme

Amino Acid Developer

- The same reagents used to develop amino acid prints on paper can be used to develop prints left in blood on porous items. NIN, DFO, and IND are colorless and do not stain the background.
- Application and development techniques are the same as for paper.

Selection of Blood Reagent

Selection of blood reagent is dependent on the type and color of the evidence to be processed. Dark-colored items should be processed with fluorescent reagents, be they nonporous or porous items. Porous items could be stained by some of the dark-colored reagents to the point that any fingerprint detail would be hidden.

Blood reagents are very sensitive and cause a strong reaction with blood prints. Normally, blood that is visible will overdevelop, so if ridge detail is visible, photograph those prints prior to processing. When applying the reagent, process a wide area around the visible blood stains and also where items are believed to have been touched. The results can be remarkable.

Miscellaneous

Blood Print Reagents

Reagent	Type	Visual/Fluorescence
ABTS (2,2'-Azino-bis(3-ethylbenzothiazoline-6-sulfonic acid)	P	V
Acid yellow 7	P	F
Amido black	P	V
Ashley's reagent	P	V
Coomassie blue	P	V
Crowle's double stain	P	V
DAB (diaminobenzydine)	H	V
DFO (1, 8-diazofluoren-9-one)	A	F
Fluorescein	A	F
LCV (leucocrystal violet)	H	V
Leucomalachite green	H	V
Merbromin	H	F
Ninhydrin	A	V
Ortho-tolidine	H	V
TMB (tetramethylbenzidine)	H	V
Some Additional (UK Police Scientific Development Branch)		
Acid Violet 19+	H	
Organic acid peroxide		
Acid black 1	P	
Acid Violet 17	P	
Lucifer yellow VS	A	F
SYPRO	A	F
Ruby protein blot stain		

A, amino acid; V, visual; H, heme; F, fluorescent; P, protein (generally 450 nm).
FDLE SOP Latent Section, CBDIAI Latent Processing guide, FBI Latent Processing Guide. Journal of Forensic Identification 55 (6), 741.

Chapter 3

Special Considerations

Chapter Outline

THERMAL PAPER

Thermal papers, mostly register tapes, pose a problem due to the background darkening when sprayed with Ninhydrin (NIN), 1,2 indanedione (IND), or 1, 8-diazofluoren-9-one (DFO). Following the instructions for Ninhydrin, using the dip method, dip and agitate the thermal paper in the Ninhydrin until the dark background is washed off (a darkening of the developer solution will occur, but this has not shown to inhibit the reagent properties of the Ninhydrin) (see Figure 1). If after drying more darkness appears, dip it in acetone (see thermal paper **destaining solution**). This process also works with IND. Use the dip method and agitate until the dark background is gone. This does not interfere with the fluorescent properties of IND or DFO. If you have already processed the item and it has resulted in the dark or black background, rinsing the item in a bath of acetone should remove the background, leaving the developed prints intact.

Note: this process basically "bleaches" the thermal paper, leaving only the developed print behind. The document should be photographed or copied front and back prior to using the destaining solution. Initial and date the document before copying or photography using a china marker (grease pencil).

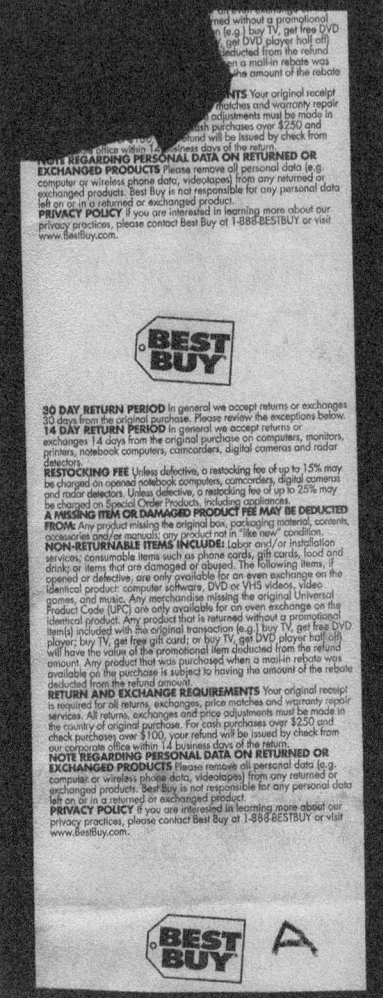

A: AFTER ACETONE WASH

FIGURE 1 Post acetone wash

These markings will survive the process, allowing for proper documentation/ chain of custody.

Certain countries or jurisdictions do not allow the original document to be altered during processing, so check with your court system prior to using this process.

Ruthenium tetroxide (RTX) can be used prior to NIN, IND, or DFO.

FINGERPRINTS ON HUMAN SKIN

No single process or sequence of processes has been proven to develop latent prints on human skin with any regularity. Ambient temperature and humidity conditions can be a major factor in recovering prints. The late Bill Sampson was a pioneer in the area of developing prints on human skin, and he likened print residue on the skin surface to bacon grease: if too cold, the residue would coagulate and would not be receptive to development. Likewise, if the residue was too warm, it might migrate to the surrounding tissue. Proper humidity can affect your outcome as well.

Some of the methods used in the past with limited success are the following:

- Iodine fume, Silver plate transfer method—iodine fume the area of skin presumed to have been touched. Place the silver plate against the fumed area and expose the silver plate to bright light. Look for bruising caused by possible grabbing or choking.
- Magnetic powder
- Cyanoacrylate fume the body
- Kromekote paper (glossy photo printer paper) transfer method. The glossy side of the paper is placed against an area of interest, removed and processed with CA (cyanoacrylate) followed by the powder method.
- Standard powder

The results: all methods to date are hit and miss.

TIPS ON PROCESSING LATEX OR NITRILE GLOVES

When first removed from the box, the bead at the wrist cuff is *rolled under*; this fact will be important later if you are identifying which side is the exterior surface. When processing gloves, you may want to use different processes on the exterior and interior surfaces. If blood traces are present, you may want to use a blood reagent on the exterior and CA on the interior. If ridge detail is developed on the exterior finger tips of the glove with the blood reagent, consider the possibility that if the glove was tight, the summits of the finger may have raised the surface of the glove tip enough for it to be coated with a thin film of blood. This would produce a duplicate of the actual finger tip and would require reversed orientation in order to be compared. (This scenario actually happened, resulting in a conviction.)

OBJECTS FROM FIRES

The techniques used to develop latent prints on fire-affected exhibits vary from substrate to substrate and, in some cases, deviate from techniques usually recommended for those substrates. Soot removal can result in exposing latent prints that have been "burned" or etched into the substrate.

Techniques for Soot Removal

Soot on paper substrates should be removed using Absorene, http://www. absorene.com/prodsumm/prod06.html, a putty-like substance rubbed gently across the surface of the exhibit.

Lifting tape is the most effective mechanical soot removal process for flat, nonporous substrates. It leaves less surface residue than other methods and does not involve wetting the exhibit, as earlier methods recommend. For nonflat or textured surfaces, the use of silicone-casting material is recommended. This is applied as a paste and then peeled off once it has dried to reveal a cleaner surface.

Soot Removal from Blood Prints

For porous substrates that have not been covered in soot, protein reagents have shown the ability to develop prints left in blood that have been exposed to temperatures of 200 °C. For porous substrates that are covered in soot, the Absorene method should be used.

For nonporous surfaces, the silicone-casting method described above is recommended. The lifting tape method is not recommended, as it may remove some of the fragile blood deposits.

RECOVERY OF FINGERPRINTS FROM KLEENEX AND TISSUE PAPER (OR SIMILAR PAPER MATERIALS SUBJECT TO DAMAGE WHEN WET PROCESSED)

Tissue or Kleenex-type material can be processed by using a dry Ninhydrin method. It is fairly simple and effective. Two pieces of copy paper are soaked with Ninhydrin and are allowed to dry. The item to be processed is then placed between the two and gently pressed with a light weight, such as a book. Allow approximately 2 h for development. After examination, if the development is weak, the item can be pressed for additional time.

RECOVERY OF LATENT PRINTS FROM ROUGH OR TEXTURED SURFACES

Recovery of latent fingerprints from rough or textured surfaces can pose the problem of not being able to get your lifting medium down into the valleys of the uneven surface. It was determined that a type of water-based glue can be poured or spread directly over a powder-processed latent print without fear of smearing or damaging the print. The glue product that produces consistently good results is made by Pentel Company, Ltd and is marketed as "Pentel Roll'n Glue," Quick Dry Liquid Adhesive, #ER 101.

The following method has been used successfully to recover latent prints from uneven surfaces using "Pentel Roll'n Glue™."
1. The glue is poured directly over the dusted latent print.
2. The glue is spread in a thin sheet evenly over the print.
3. The glue is allowed to air dry for approximately 5–10 min, or a hand hair drier can be used to gently accelerate the process. Care must be taken not to overheat the glue. Lifting the glue before it is dry will ruin the lift.
4. The glue with the latent print can be lifted by placing ordinary lifting tape over the glue and slowly peeling the tape and glue off the surface. Place the lifted combination on a contrasting backer card.

Another product, Accutrans®, has been marketed for just this purpose. The material is polyvinylsiloxane, a compound used in the dental profession to take impressions in the mouth. This material has been used by forensic professionals for a number of years to take impressions of tool marks. Recently, Accutrans® developed a transparent compound that is used similarly to the glue process. This material is dispensed from a tube that holds two compounds, one of which is a hardener. The two are mixed as they travel down the tip of the tube, and the mix is applied to the area of interest. The resulting mold is very pliable and, in the case of the transparent formula, can be used to lift powdered prints from uneven surfaces.

Several forensic supply firms offer a lifting tape with a thick adhesive that reportedly can be worked into the textured surface.

RECOVERY OF FINGERPRINTS FROM DESICCATED REMAINS

Fingerprint standards from desiccated remains can be difficult to recover because the skin takes on a corrugated texture and looses pliability. The normal process is removing the epidermal skin and placing it over a gloved finger or using a syringe to inject a saline solution under the dermis then inking and rolling. Casting the ends of the fingers with Mikrosil™, Durocast™, polyvinylsiloxane, or Accutrans® can greatly increase the success of your recovery attempts. A thin casting of the finger by one of the aforementioned materials results in a pliable reproduction that can be flattened and photographed using oblique lighting.

RECOVERY OF FINGERPRINTS FROM WET OR SUBMERGED EVIDENCE

Too often, items that are recovered from a pond or lake are not considered for fingerprint processing. The same holds true for items that have been subjected to rain. This is another instance where the makeup of the matrix allows for an opportunity that a latent may still exist. Small Particle Reagent for nonporous and Physical Developer for porous are two processes that can be used on previously wet items. Also, once the items have dried, additional processes for lipid residue can be tried (Iodine fuming and Cyanoacrylate fuming, for example). Objects that are recovered from moving water, such as a stream, have less of a chance for recovery due to the scrubbing action of the water, but an attempt should still be made.

TOUCH DNA

DNA has become a very important compliment to fingerprints, as are all advances in the forensic field. Touch DNA is defined as the body fluids or epithelial cells left behind on an object when it is handled by a suspect. The advances in touch DNA recovery has complicated fingerprint development to a certain extent, as we are now posed with a question: are we going to go after fingerprint or DNA recovery as some fingerprint processes preclude the recovery of DNA? Biology labs are slowly learning to recover DNA, even after certain fingerprint development processes have been used. The list of these processes is growing, and when the question "DNA or fingerprints" arises, a conference with the DNA analyst is recommended. Biology can work with very small samples, and a meeting with the DNA analyst may result in both types of processing being carried out.

RECOVERY OF FINGERPRINTS FROM FIREARMS

Firearms, cartridges, and casings (fired cartridges) present some unique problems for the analyst. In theory, the surfaces should be ideal for fingerprint development with powders or cyanoacrylate, but due to methods of concealment, the firearm will probably be carried in a pocket or holster, which has a tendency to wipe the surfaces clean. Long guns are least affected by this, followed by revolvers where certain areas on the cylinder, etc., are protected. On semiautomatic handguns, however, most surfaces are exposed or unsuitable for fingerprint recovery. Consider the trigger and hammer are knurled and the grips are checkered; while not suitable for fingerprints, these areas are prime areas for touch DNA. Firearms are also coated with a light film of oil in the protected areas. CA fuming, followed by dye staining and observation under the forensic light source, is the most productive process for firearms such as it is.

Cartridges can produce results due to its surface type. First, they are smooth, hard, and protected inside the weapon. Second, if they are brass, fingerprints may be etched into the surface by acids contained in perspiration. The same can be said for casings, except that the heat generated by the powder detonation has a tendency to degrade results. CA fuming, followed by gun bluing techniques, is the most productive.

Processing cartridges and casings can preclude some examinations by firearms examiners, such as ejector or magazine marks, so a consultation with them is recommended.

Study: Success of Latent Print Development Processes on Firearms, Cartridges, and Casings

On October 15, 2008, I started a study of the success of latent print development on firearms, cartridges, and casings. Our forensic technologist recorded the results of processing firearms, cartridges, and casings as they were returned to the evidence vault. He gathered this information from the analysts' reports and case files.

183 firearms, 1212 cartridges, and 269 casings were processed over a one-year period. The results are as follows:

16 latent prints were developed on firearms and magazines (or 8.7%).
Two latent prints were developed on cartridges (0.1%).
One latent print was developed on a casing (0.3%).

For the most part, the items were subjected to visual, cyanoacrylate fuming, MBD (7-P methoxybenzylamino-4-nitrobenz-2 OXA-1-3-diazole) dye staining, and in some cases, powder processing. Gun blue was also used to process cartridges and casings in a small number of cases.

I completed this test primarily to answer the question of how often or how many weapons we actually develop latent prints on.

There is obviously room for improvement, and we have been trying prefuming with glacial acetic acid and ammonia with mixed results. The brand and type of CA has been shown to affect the success of CA fuming in a study by the Israelis; their study also investigates other types of processing.

Senior Crime Laboratory Analyst.
Stephen P. Kasper

ADDITIONAL PROCESSES AND TECHNIQUES

Cy-Vac

The Cy-Vac polymerizes the latent impression using cyanoacrylate in a heated, vacuum environment. The vacuum will eliminate background moisture and will allow the cyanoacrylate to attach to the components of the latent impression, thus eliminating the overfuming of an item of evidence, which may occur with manual cyanoacrylate techniques. Numerous materials, including plastic bags, weapons, metals, and various other substrates, may be processed using the Cy-Vac. Cyanoacrylate shall be used as a preliminary process when utilizing subsequent processing techniques. Fluorescent dye staining, in conjunction with laser examinations, is dependent on the proper use of cyanoacrylate fuming techniques.

Vacuum Metal Deposition

Vacuum metal deposition (VMD) has many commercial applications, including coating reflective surfaces, the antireflection coating of camera lenses, and the production of semiconductors. For normal commercial coating purposes, the surface to be coated is first thoroughly cleaned, as the deposition process is extremely sensitive to surface contamination. It is this sensitivity, however, which provides the key to applying this technique to fingerprint detection.

After an exhibit is placed inside the chamber, a small quantity of gold (4–5 mg) and several grams of zinc are loaded into separate evaporation dishes located under the exhibit. Pumps then reduce pressure to operating levels. Gold is evaporated by passing a high current from low voltage through the evaporation dish. This results in a very minute deposition of gold over the entire exhibit surface facing the dish. It is suspected that the gold actually absorbs into any fingerprint residue present. Zinc is then evaporated and deposited in a similar fashion. Zinc will generally condense only onto another metal, so it adheres to the gold coated background and valleys between the fingerprint ridges. The technique is very sensitive and will detect monolayers of lipid material. In this way, a visible fingerprint is developed that can then be photographed for a permanent record.

Hyperspectral Imaging

Latent fingerprints (those left on an object by touch, as opposed to fingerprints recorded by ink or other means) at a crime scene usually require some method to be visualized, such as the application of a powder or chemicals or a reading by specialized imaging equipment. Hyperspectral imaging—the capture of hundreds of narrow spectral bands typically on a single detector, as opposed to multispectral, or the capture of several broadband channels on multiple detectors—can enhance the detection of latent fingerprints and improve specificity without physical contact or damage to the prints. Hyperspectral imaging allows a forensic scientist to analyze and identify not only the fingerprint, but potentially any material left between the ridges of the fingerprint. For forensic applications, extensive chemical or spectral libraries are maintained for a wide range of material sets. By scanning through the hyperspectral data, an analyst is better able to view contrast differences from wavelength to wavelength that may help to identify specific ridge patterns of the fingerprint.

Reflected Ultra Violet Imaging System (RUVIS)

Shortwave UV light is directed at the substrate to be examined. UV light is either reflected or absorbed by the matrix residues present in the fingerprint. A lens focuses this reflected and scattered UV light through a UV filter, which is then enhanced, converting it into a visible latent print. The background appears black, as most materials absorb shortwave UV light, leaving only the print visible.

Chapter 4

Process Sequence Protocols

Chapter Outline

FUNDAMENTALS

Every fingerprint is a printed copy of the ridge detail present on the palmar or plantar surfaces of the hands and feet. In order for a printed copy to be produced, some material (matrix) must be transferred from the summits of the ridges to a substrate. Sometimes the prints are invisible or *latent*, as the matrix is made up of a material that is transparent such as sweat or body oils. Sometimes they are visible or *patent*, as the matrix consists of materials such as grease, paint, or blood. Sometimes they are *plastic*, or visible, because the fingers have been placed in a material that is sticky or pliable, such as tacky paint or putty, and leave a "3-D" print.

For the last two scenarios, the only process required is to "recover" the prints by photography or casting.

For the first scenario, however, steps must be taken to make the "invisible" prints visible. Since the introduction of fingerprint identification to the US at the Worlds Fair in St. Louis in 1904, our discipline has developed many methods to accomplish this task.

Correct processing techniques increase the probability of developing the best quality latent prints. Following the sequences listed in this guide ensures the best opportunity to develop all latent prints on an item, no matter what the matrix or substrate is.

Surfaces on which latent prints are deposited can be divided into two basic categories—porous and nonporous. The following pages list the recommended sequential processes for porous, nonporous, semiporous, and some unique and/or difficult surfaces.

The following are the recommended processes and sequence of application for a particular substrate.

Depending on the circumstances, all of the processes might not be performed. This is left to the discretion of the forensic professional.

Process sequences are listed for the following substrates. These represent a cross section of the types of items processed and can be adapted to fit most materials.

Latent Print Processing Guide. http://dx.doi.org/10.1016/B978-0-12-803507-8.00004-3

Porous
Bloodstained specimens
Rubber gloves
Tape (adhesive side)
Photographs

Nonporous
Cardboard
Tape (nonadhesive side)
Wallpaper
Glossy paper

Porous surfaces
1. Visual
2. Inherent fluorescence by laser or alternate light source*
3. RTX (ruthenium tetroxide)
4. Iodine fuming
5. DFO (1,8-diazafluoren-9-one) or IND (1,2-indanedione)
6. Laser or alternate light source
7. Ninhydrin, following ninhydrin if required zinc chloride (fluorescent) (see thermal paper tips in chapter 3)
8. Physical developer or silver nitrate
* Alternate light source includes ultraviolet (UV) light.

Nonporous surfaces
1. Visual
2. Inherent fluorescence by laser or alternate light source
3. RTX
4. Cyanoacrylate fuming
5. Laser or alternate light source
6. Cyanoacrylate dye
7. Laser or alternate light source
8. Powder

Bloodstained specimens—porous
1. Visual
2. Inherent fluorescence by laser or alternate light source
3. DFO (1,8-diazafluoren-9-one), IND (1,2-indanedione)
4. Laser or alternate light source
5. Ninhydrin
6. Leucocrystal violet (LCV)
7. Diaminobenzidine (DAB)
8. Physical developer

Bloodstained specimens—nonporous
1. Visual
2. Inherent fluorescence by laser or alternate light source
3. Amido black; if not available, use coomassie blue or diaminobenzidine (DAB), Acid yellow 7 (for dark surfaces), or others (see Processes Table of Contents)
4. Cyanoacrylate fuming
5. Laser or alternate light source
6. Cyanoacrylate dye

7. Laser or alternate light source
8. Powder

Cardboard
1. Visual
2. Inherent fluorescence by laser or alternate light source
3. DFO (1,8-diazafluoren-9-one) or IND (1,2-indanedione)
4. Laser or alternate light source
5. Ninhydrin
6. Silver nitrate or physical developer

Rubber gloves—semiporous
1. Visual
2. Inherent fluorescence by laser or alternate light source
3. Iodine fuming
4. Cyanoacrylate fuming
5. Laser or alternate light source
6. Magnetic powder
7. Cyanoacrylate dye
8. Laser or alternate light source
9. Ninhydrin
10. Distilled water rinse
11. Physical developer

Tape

When processing the nonadhesive side of tape, the integrity of the adhesive side should not be compromised by contact with cyanoacrylate dyes or other solvents. Acetate or some other substrate should be used to protect the adhesive side.

Often tape is submitted to the lab in a "ball" or overlapped and needs to be separated. Some of the methods to separate the tape are freezing, liquid nitrogen, or commercially available products such as "Un-do."

Tape—nonadhesive side
1. Visual
2. Inherent fluorescence by laser or alternate light source
3. Cyanoacrylate fuming
4. Laser or alternate light source
5. Cyanoacrylate dye
6. Laser or alternate light source
7. Powder

Tape—adhesive side
Light-colored adhesive side of tape
1. Visual
2. Inherent fluorescence by laser or alternate light source
3. RTX

   4. Sticky-side powder, gentian violet (crystal violet), or Wetwop

   5. Laser or alternate light source

Dark-colored adhesive side of tape

1. Visual

2. Inherent fluorescence by laser or alternate light source

3. Sticky-side powder, Tape-Glo*, gentian violet, or Wetwop

4. Laser or alternate light source

* Cyanoacrylate fuming must be done on the nonadhesive side of tape, and then both sides can be processed with Tape-Glo.

Wallpaper

1. Visual

2. Inherent fluorescence by laser or alternate light source

3. RTX

4. Iodine fuming

5. Ninhydrin

6. Silver nitrate or physical developer

Photographs—emulsion side

1. Visual

2. Inherent fluorescence by laser or alternate light source

3. RTX

4. Iodine fuming

5. Cyanoacrylate fuming

6. Laser or alternate light source

7. Cyanoacrylate dye

8. Laser or alternate light source

9. Powder

Photographs—paper side—semiporous

  1. Visual

  2. Inherent fluorescence by laser or alternate light source

  3. RTX

  4. Cyanoacrylate fuming

  5. Laser or alternate light source

  6. Magnetic powder

  7. DFO (1,8-diazafluoren-9-one) or IND (1,2-indanedione)

  8. Laser or alternate light source

  9. Ninhydrin

10. Cyanoacrylate dye

11. Laser or alternate light source

12. Physical developer

Glossy paper—semiporous

  1. Visual

  2. Inherent fluorescence by laser or alternate light source

3. RTX
4. Cyanoacrylate fuming
5. Laser or alternate light source
6. Magnetic powder
7. DFO (1,8-diazafluoren-9-one) or IND (1,2-indanedione)
8. Laser or alternate light source
9. Ninhydrin
10. Cyanoacrylate dye
11. Laser or alternate light source
12. Physical developer

This list of processes is grouped by their use on a particular substrate or type of matrix and their position in the proper sequence.

Porous
1. RTX
2. Iodine fuming
3. DFO or IND (1,2-indanedione)
4. Forensic light source examination
5. Ninhydrin, optional post treatment with zinc chloride
6. Physical developer or silver nitrate

Nonporous
1. RTX
2. Cyanoacrylate fuming followed by a **dye stain** and forensic light source examination
3. Dye stains (use one):
   > Ardrox
   > Basic red 28
   > Basic yellow 40
   > Fluorescent dye pink
   > MBD
   > M-Star RAM
   > Rhodamine 6G Aqueous
   > Rhodamine 6G Methanol
   > Safranin-O
4. Powders and particulates
5. Heat/flame particulates
6. Lifting materials

Fluorescent surface—inherent or dye stained
   Forensic light sources

Blood reagents
1. Acid yellow 7
2. Amido black 10B (methanol)
3. Amido black 10B (aqueous)

4. Ashley's reagent
5. Coomassie brilliant blue R250
6. Crowle's double stain
7. DAB
8. DFO or IND (1,2-indanedione)
9. Fluorescein
10. Ninhydrin
11. Leucocrystal violet
12. Tetramethylbenzidine (TMB)

Cartridge cases—unfired rounds or spent casings
1. Cyanoacrylate fuming
2. Liquid gun blue
3. Dye stain and FLS examination (see nonporous above)
4. Powders and particulates

Footwear
1. Potassium thiocyanate
2. Powders and particulates
3. Silicone rubber casting
4. Dental stone cast

Adhesive surfaces
1. Sticky-side powder
2. Crystal violet
3. Tape-Glo
4. Wetwop
5. RTX

Plastic or 3-D prints
1. Silicone rubber casting
2. Photo

Wet or previously wet nonporous
   Small particle reagent

Wet or previously wet porous
   Physical developer

Greasy/waxy
   Sudan black

Miscellaneous
   Luminol, RTX, thermal paper destaining solution

Chapter 5

The Processes

Chapter Outline

It is recommended that the SWGFAST (Scientific Working Group on Friction Ridge Analysis, Study and Technology) guidelines for validation be followed for all *novel, modified, or newly implemented* techniques that pertain to casework.

Note: Technically SWGFAST (Scientific Working Group on Friction Ridge Analysis, Study, and Technology) no longer exists. It has been replaced by OSAC—FRS (Organization of Scientific Area Committees—Friction Ridge Subcommittee). As of now, OSAC is still using SWGFAST standards.

DOCUMENT #17

Standard for the Validation and Performance Review of Friction Ridge Impression Development and Examination Techniques (Latent/Tenprint)

1. Preamble
   1.1. This document provides direction for validating technical procedures or methods (hereafter referred to as "techniques") prior to being introduced into operational casework. This document also provides direction for the performance check of technical procedures and methods prior to the techniques being deployed in their operational setting.
   1.2. Validation assesses the ability of techniques to meet specified objectives, their benefits and limitations, and the optimal conditions under which results can be obtained. Performance check assesses the ability of techniques to meet specified objectives and verify the optimal conditions under which results can be obtained.
   1.3. Validation and performance check are part of scientific best practices, quality assurance procedures, and laboratory accreditation requirements.
2. Scope

These guidelines apply to all *novel, modified, or newly implemented tech-niques* that pertain to casework.

Refer to the complete SWGFAST document #17 at (http://www.swgfast. org/documents/validation/121124_Validation-Performance-Review_2.0.pdf).

Note: Some of the following techniques are available already mixed from forensic materials distributors, including some of the more popular processes such as Ninhydrin, Amido black, and many dye stains.

Acid Yellow 7

Category: Stain (reagent)

Reacts with: Blood protein

Process product: Fluorescent orange-colored stain where contact is made with blood protein

Color

PURPOSE

The purpose of this process is to develop bloody fingerprints on dark surfaces both porous and nonporous, which will fluoresce when exposed to 450–500 nm light from a forensic light source.

MATERIALS

A) 5-Sulfosalicylic acid

B) Distilled water

C) Acid Yellow 7

D) Glacial acetic acid

E) Methanol

F) Ethanol

G) Glass beakers and trays

H) Magnetic stirrer

I) Forensic light source

MIXING PROCEDURE

Sulfosalicylic acid fixing solution

46 g of 5-Sulfosalicylic acid

2000 ml distilled water

Place 46 g of 5-Sulfosalicylic acid in a clean, dry 3 l glass beaker. Add 2000 ml of distilled water to the 46 g of 5-Sulfosalicylic acid while stirring with a magnetic stirrer. Once the 46 g of 5-Sulfosalicylic acid has been completely dissolved, place the fixing solution into a 2 l glass storage bottle.

Methanol Fixing Solution

50 ml glacial acetic acid

450 ml methanol

Mix glacial acetic acid and methanol in a glass beaker and store in a glass or plastic storage bottle.

Working Solution

> 2 g Acid Yellow 7
> 100 ml acetic acid
> 500 ml ethanol
> 1400 ml distilled water

Combine, in order, the above listed items in a clean, dry 3 l glass beaker. Stir with a magnetic stirrer for at least 30 min. Place the working solution into a 2 l glass storage bottle.

Wash Solution

> 100 ml acetic acid
> 500 ml ethanol
> 1400 ml distilled water

Combine, in order, the above listed items in a clean, dry 3 l glass beaker. A colorless wash solution will result. Place the wash solution into a 2 l glass storage bottle.

The shelf life for the above solutions is at least 6 months.

PROCESSING PROCEDURE

A) Fix or stabilize the blood on the surface of the evidence to prevent the blood print from running.
B) Immerse the article containing the impression in a glass tray of the blood fixing solution for 5 min.
C) The standard heat fixing and methanol fixing methods can also be used.

Apply the Staining (Working) Solution

Immerse the article containing the fixed impression in a tray of the working solution for 5–10 min.

Wash Solution

Immerse the article containing the impression in a tray of wash solution and rock gently until excess dye has been removed from the background and the greatest contrast has been achieved.

(Gently flooding the surface of the article using a wash bottle can also be used to apply the various solutions.)

Observe the results by exposing to electromagnetic energy produced by a forensic light source in the 450–500 nm range and observe using an orange barrier filter.

Low contrast fingerprints may be improved by retreatment with working and wash solutions.

SAFETY CONSIDERATIONS

A) Refer to Material Safety Data Sheets (MSDS) for specified chemicals.
B) Follow proper safety precautions.
C) Use proper ventilation.
D) Wear suitable protective clothing, gloves, and goggles.
E) Avoid contact with skin and eyes.

LIMITATION

The process is water-based and care should be taken not to expose items that will be damaged by water. Acid Yellow 7 is a protein dye and will not develop fingerprints with a normal body fluid matrix.

RESULTS

Fingerprints fluoresce brightly under the 450 nm wave length setting on the forensic light source and are just slightly less bright at the 455 nm setting. Acid Yellow 7 is an excellent choice for processing dark items for the presence of blood prints. There are not many processes to choose from when faced with bloody fingerprints on a black or dark surface. The standard blood reagents develop dark-colored ridges, which are difficult to see or photograph. Some of the other options for developing fluorescent blood prints (fluorescein or merbromine, etc.) are harder to use and do not result in fluorescence as strong as Acid Yellow 7.

QUALITY CONTROL

All reagent "working" solutions should be quality control tested at the time they are prepared. They should also be tested daily or prior to use on actual evidence. This quality control testing is to insure the accuracy of the mixture and that the desired reaction is being obtained.

LITERATURE REFERENCES

Home Office, Police Scientific Development Branch, Manual of Fingerprint Development Techniques, second edition, revised January 2001, second revision August 2004, Chapter 4, Acid Yellow 7, pp. 6–9.
Amanda L. Atkins, Development of Bloody Latent Prints on Dark Surfaces. CCSI, United States Army Criminal Investigation Laboratory. http://www.oninonin.com/fp/2007jul27_USACIL_acid_yellow_presentation.pdf.

> **Amido Black 10B (Methanol Base)**
> Category: Stain (reagent)
> Reacts with: Blood protein
> Process product: Blue–black colored stain where amido makes contact with blood protein
> Color ▮▮▮▮▮▮

PURPOSE

Amido Black is used for the development or enhancement of latent prints, footwear, and tire impressions in suspected blood containing protein residue on porous and nonporous items.

MATERIALS

A) Naphthol Blue Black (also known as Amido Black 10B or Buffalo Black NBR)
B) Glacial acetic acid
C) Methanol (also known as methyl alcohol)
D) Scale, beakers, graduated cylinder, magnetic stirrer and stirring bar, and clear or dark bottles for storage
E) Wash bottles, trays, and sprayer

MIXING PROCEDURE

Developer Solution

1 g Naphthol Blue Black
50 ml glacial acetic acid
450 ml methanol

Combine the glacial acetic acid with methanol and mix on a stirring device. Add the Naphthol Blue Black and allow the ingredients to stir until the Naphthol Blue Black is dissolved. This should take approximately 15–30 min.

Rinse Solution

100 ml glacial acetic acid
900 ml methanol

Combine the glacial acetic acid with the methanol. This mixture can be mixed with a stirring bar or manually.

PROCESSING PROCEDURE

A) All visible prints or impressions of potential value in blood should be photographed prior to processing.

B) Prior to application, the suspected blood should be completely dry or fixed on the item to be processed.

C) Apply the developer to the specimen by dipping, spraying, or the use of a wash bottle.

D) Completely cover the target area until the desired development has been obtained.

E) Rinse the target area with the rinse solution to remove the background stain.

F) These steps can be repeated to improve the development and contrast.

G) If the background color is still too intense, the rinse may be applied again.

H) Allow the specimen to air-dry.

I) All prints or impressions of potential value should be photographed.

SAFETY CONSIDERATIONS

A) Refer to MSDS for specified chemicals.

B) Use proper ventilation.

C) Avoid contact with skin and eyes.

D) Wear suitable protective clothing, gloves, and goggles.

E) Follow proper safety precautions.

LIMITATION

The use of Amido Black is limited to items that are contaminated with suspected blood.

QUALITY CONTROL

All reagent "working" solutions should be quality control tested at the time they are prepared. They should also be tested daily or prior to use on actual evidence. This quality control testing is to insure the accuracy of the mixture and that the desired reaction is being obtained.

LITERATURE REFERENCES

Boyd, Fred M., January 1990, Bloody Footwear Impression Enhanced by a Chemical Reaction. Florida Division of the International Association for Identification Newsletter, pp. 4–5.

Federal Bureau of Investigation. Chemical Formulas and Processing Guide for Developing Latent Prints, pp. 11–12, revised 1999.

Federal Bureau of Investigation. Use of Hazardous Substances in the Latent Fingerprint Laboratory, pp. 1–6.

Hamm, Ernest, 1983. Enhancement and Development of Blood Prints. In: Paper Presented to the Georgia State Division of the International Association for Identification, pp. 1–12.

Technical Note on Amido Black. Lightning Powder Company, Inc., pp. 1–4.

Amido Black 10B (Water-Based Formula)
Category: Stain (reagent)
Reacts with: Blood protein
Process product: Blue–black colored stain where amido makes contact with blood protein
Color ████████

PURPOSE

Amido Black is used for the development or enhancement of latent prints, footwear, and tire impressions in suspected blood containing protein residue on porous and nonporous items. The Amido Black water-based formula is used in place of the methanol-based formula when there may be a question about or a problem using a solvent base with a painted surface.

MIXING PROCEDURE

Citric Acid Stock Solution

> 38 g citric acid
> 2 l distilled water

Combine the above ingredients and place on a stirring device until the citric acid is dissolved.

Developer Solution

> 1 l citric acid stock solution
> 2 g Naphthol Blue Black (Amido Black)
> 2 ml Kodak Photo-Flo 600 Solution

Combine the above ingredients by placing the liter of citric acid stock solution on a stirring device. Slowly add the 2 g of Naphthol Blue Black, stirring for approximately 30 min. Add the Photo-Flo 600 and stir lightly by hand.

Rinse Solution

> 1 l citric acid stock solution

PROCESSING PROCEDURE

A) All visible prints or impressions of potential value in blood should be photographed prior to processing.

B) Prior to application, the suspected blood should be completely dry or fixed on the item to be processed.

C) Apply the developer to the specimen by dipping, spraying, or through the use of a wash bottle.

D) Completely cover the target area until the desired development has been obtained.

E) Rinse the target area with the rinse solution to remove the background stain.

F) These steps can be repeated to improve the development and contrast.

G) After maximum clarity is achieved, apply the rinse solution again.

H) Allow the item to air-dry.

I) All prints or impressions of potential value should be photographed.

SAFETY CONSIDERATIONS

A) Refer to MSDS for specified chemicals.

B) Use proper ventilation.

C) Avoid contact with skin and eyes.

D) Wear suitable protective clothing, gloves, and goggles.

E) Follow proper safety precautions.

LIMITATION

The use of Amido Black is limited to items that are contaminated with suspected blood.

QUALITY CONTROL

All reagent "working" solutions should be quality control tested at the time they are prepared. They should also be tested daily or prior to use on actual evidence. This quality control testing is to insure the accuracy of the mixture and that the desired reaction is being obtained.

LITERATURE REFERENCES

Boyd, Fred M., January 1990. Bloody Footwear Impression Enhanced by a Chemical Reaction. Florida Division of the International Association for Identification Newsletter, pp. 4–5.

Federal Bureau of Investigation. Chemical Formulas and Processing Guide for Developing Latent Prints, pp. 11–12, revised 1999.

Federal Bureau of Investigation. Use of Hazardous Substances in the Latent Fingerprint Laboratory, pp. 1–6.

Hamm, Ernest, 1983: Enhancement and Development of Blood Prints. In: Paper Presented to the Georgia State Division of the International Association for Identification, pp. 1–12.

Technical Note on Amido Black. Lightning Powder Company, Inc., pp. 1–4.

Ardrox

Category: Dye stain
Reacts with: Bonds to cyanoacrylate (CA) residue
Process product: Fluorescent yellow stain adheres to CA residue that has polymerized to fingerprint matrix
Color [   ]

PURPOSE

Ardrox is a luminescent dye used to make cyanoacrylate-developed latent prints more visible on various colored surfaces. This dye is used in conjunction with a long-wave ultraviolet or forensic light source.

MATERIALS

A) Ardrox
B) Methanol, ethyl alcohol, or acetone
C) Tap water
D) Graduated cylinder, beaker, and storage container
E) Forensic light source

MIXING PROCEDURE

0.3% Solution

30 ml ardrox
1000 ml methanol, ethyl alcohol, or acetone

Mix thoroughly. Solution mixes easily in storage container, no stir plate is necessary.

*Ardrox can be mixed with different concentration levels by adjusting the amount of ardrox added to the methanol.

PROCESSING PROCEDURE

A) Fume evidence with cyanoacrylate.
B) Dip, swab, or spray the dye staining solution over surface.
C) Wait a few seconds, then rinse thoroughly using tap water (*rinsing with water is optional*).
D) Air-dry or accelerate drying with a hair dryer.
E) Examine using a forensic light source, including, but not limited to, wavelengths from 365 to 450 nm.
F) Photograph all prints of potential value.
G) If no usable latent prints are apparent and the dye adheres to the background, rinse surface with an alcohol wash and reexamine.

H) If dye has been removed, reapply the dye stain after evidence has thoroughly dried.

I) If dye is still adhering to the background, rinse a second time using alcohol-soaked cotton balls, wiping the surface.

J) Reapply dye stain if necessary.

K) All prints of potential value should be photographed.

SAFETY CONSIDERATIONS

A) Refer to MSDS for specified chemicals.

B) Use in fume hood when applying the stain.

C) Use proper safety equipment such as protective clothing, gloves, and goggles.

D) Follow proper safety precautions.

E) When examining the evidence with a light source, wear protective goggles.

LIMITATION

The use of ardrox is limited to nonporous surfaces that have been previously processed with cyanoacrylate.

QUALITY CONTROL

All reagent "working" solutions should be quality control tested at the time they are prepared. They should also be tested daily or prior to use on actual evidence. This quality control testing is to insure the accuracy of the mixture and that the desired reaction is being obtained.

LITERATURE REFERENCES

Federal Bureau of Investigation. Chemical Formulas and Processing Guide for Developing Latent Prints, pp. 47–48.

Technical Note on Ardrox Fluorescent Dye. Lightning Powder Company, Inc.

McCarthy, M., 1990. Evaluation of Ardrox as a luminescent stain for cyanoacrylate processed latent impressions. Journal of Forensic Identification 40 (2), pp 75–80.

Miles, C., 1987. Analysis of Ardrox 970-P10 Liquid Penetrant. Field Identification Resource Section Report #001, Ottawa, Ontario.

Olenik, John H., 1992. An alternate solvent system. Kodak Tech Bits (1), pp. 14–15.

Ashley's Reagent

Category: Reagent
Reacts with: Protein
Process product: Visible purple stain
Color ████████

PURPOSE

Ashley's Reagent is a commercially prepared product used for the enhancement of latent prints, footwear, and tire impressions in suspected blood containing protein residue on porous and nonporous items. This reagent is not specific for blood but is for the enhancement of blood protein.

MATERIALS

A) Ashley's Reagent
B) Trays and "tissue" paper

MIXING PROCEDURE

Commercially prepared product

PROCESSING PROCEDURE

A) All visible prints or impressions of potential value in suspected blood should be photographed prior to processing.
B) Prior to application, the suspected blood should be completely dry or fixed on the item to be processed.
C) Apply the reagent to the specimen by the "tissue method" or by immersing the item for approximately 2 min.
D) Carefully rinse the target area with tap water.
E) Carefully blot excess water.
F) Allow the specimen to air-dry.
G) All prints or impressions of potential value should be photographed.

SAFETY CONSIDERATIONS

A) Refer to MSDS.
B) Use proper ventilation.
C) Avoid contact with skin and eyes.
D) Wear suitable protective clothing, gloves, and goggles.
E) Follow proper safety precautions.

LIMITATION

The use of Ashley's Reagent is limited to items that are contaminated with suspected blood.

QUALITY CONTROL

All reagent "working" solutions should be quality control tested at the time they are prepared. They should also be tested daily or prior to use on actual evidence. This quality control testing is to insure the accuracy of the mixture and that the desired reaction is being obtained.

LITERATURE REFERENCES

Federal Bureau of Investigation. Use of Hazardous Substances in the Latent Fingerprint Laboratory, pp. 1–6.

Directions for use of Ashley's Reagent supplied by Forensic Research and Supply Corporation.

Basic Red 28

Category: Dye stain
Reacts with: Bonds to cyanoacrylate residue
Process product: Fluorescent red stain adheres to CA residue that has polymerized to fingerprint matrix
Color ████████████

PURPOSE

Basic Red 28 is a luminescent dye used to make cyanoacrylate-developed latent prints more visible on various colored surfaces. This dye is used in conjunction with a forensic light source.

MATERIALS

A) Basic Red 28
B) Propanol
C) Acetonitrile
D) Petroleum ether
E) Distilled water
F) Dark brown glass jar
G) Scale, beakers, graduated cylinder, magnetic stirrer, and stirring bar
H) Forensic light source
I) Wash bottles and trays

MIXING PROCEDURE

Basic Red 28 Solution

Stock Solution

> 0.2 g Basic Red 28
> 60 ml propanol
> 40 ml acetonitrile

Using a magnetic stirrer and a stirring bar, dissolve Basic Red 28 in propanol and then add acetonitrile.

Working Solution

> 5 ml stock solution
> 95 ml petroleum ether

Using a magnetic stirrer and a stirring bar, dilute the stock solution with petroleum ether.

Mix and use these solutions in a fume hood. Store the liquids in dark brown glass jars with tight-fitting lids.

PROCESSING PROCEDURE

A) Lightly fume the evidence with cyanoacrylate or in a vacuum chamber.
B) In a fume hood, apply the Basic Red 28 solution by submerging the evidence in a tray or container. Washing the solution over the surface using a chemical wash bottle can also be done.
C) After the item has dried, rinse it with distilled water to remove any background staining.
D) Allow the item to air-dry before examining it with a light source.
E) Examine the item with a forensic light source.
F) All prints or impressions of potential value should be photographed.

SAFETY CONSIDERATIONS

A) Refer to MSDS for specified chemicals.
B) The solution should be mixed and used in a fume hood.
C) Protective clothing, gloves, and goggles should be worn.
D) When examining the evidence with a light source, use the proper goggles.
E) Follow proper safety precautions.

LIMITATION

The use of Basic Red 28 is limited to nonporous surfaces that have been previously processed with cyanoacrylate.

QUALITY CONTROL

All reagent "working" solutions should be quality control tested at the time they are prepared. They should also be tested daily or prior to use on actual evidence. This quality control testing is to insure the accuracy of the mixture and that the desired reaction is being obtained.

LITERATURE REFERENCE

Technical Note on Basic Red 28. Lightning Powder Company, Inc.

Basic Yellow 40

Category: Dye stain
Reacts with: Bonds to cyanoacrylate residue
Process product: Fluorescent yellow stain adheres to CA residue that has polymerized to fingerprint matrix

Color [   ]

PURPOSE

Basic Yellow 40 (Maxilon Flavine 10GFF) is a highly luminescent dye stain that stains cyanoacrylate-developed latent prints. When illuminated with a forensic light source, latent prints luminesce brightly, and weakly developed latent prints that could not be seen under normal viewing conditions may be easily seen and photographed.

MATERIALS

A) Basic Yellow 40
B) Reagent alcohol
C) Tap water
D) Scale, beakers, and a graduated cylinder
E) Forensic light source
F) Wash bottles and trays

MIXING PROCEDURE

> 2 g Basic Yellow 40
> 1000 ml Reagent alcohol

Using a magnetic stirrer and a stirring bar, dissolve Basic Yellow 40 in alcohol. This dilution can be adjusted to make it stronger or weaker by regulating the amount of Basic Yellow 40.

PROCESSING PROCEDURE

A) Before using a solution of Basic Yellow 40, it is necessary to superglue fume the evidence. It is recommended to underfume rather than overfume. A vacuum chamber could also be used.
B) In a fume hood, apply the Basic Yellow 40 solution by submerging the evidence in a tray or container. "Washing" the solution over the surface using a chemical wash bottle can also be done.
C) Leave the solution on the surface for about 1 min.
D) Rinse the item with running tap water.
E) Allow the item to air-dry before examining with a forensic light source.

F) Using a forensic light source, examine the evidence using 450–480 nm wavelength of light and view with orange goggles. Also examine the evidence with 365 nm wavelength of light and view with clear goggles.

G) All prints of potential value should be photographed.

SAFETY CONSIDERATIONS

A) Refer to MSDS for specified chemicals.

B) The solution should be mixed and used in a fume hood.

C) Protective clothing, gloves, and goggles should be worn.

D) When examining the evidence with a light source, use the proper goggles.

E) Follow proper safety precautions.

LIMITATION

The use of Basic Yellow 40 is limited to nonporous surfaces that have been previously processed with cyanoacrylate.

QUALITY CONTROL

All reagent "working" solutions should be quality control tested at the time they are prepared. They should also be tested daily or prior to use on actual evidence. This quality control testing is to insure the accuracy of the mixture and that the desired reaction is being obtained.

LITERATURE REFERENCE

Technical Note on Basic Yellow 40. Lightning Powder Company, Inc.

BLOOD FIXERS

PURPOSE

Blood fixing is necessary to prevent the inadvertent loss of blood evidence by fingerprint processing. Using chemical techniques or heat stabilizes the blood to the substrate.

MATERIALS

A) 5-Sulfosaliclic acid
B) Methanol
C) Glacial acetic acid
D) Distilled water
E) Laboratory oven

MIXING PROCEDURE

Sulfosalicylic Acid Fixing Solution

> 46 g of 5-Sulfosalicylic acid
> 2000 ml distilled water

Place 46 g of 5-Sulfosalicylic acid in a clean, dry 3 l glass beaker. Add 2000 ml of distilled water to the 46 g of 5-Sulfosalicylic acid while stirring with a magnetic stirrer. Once the 46 g of 5-Sulfosalicylic acid has been completely dissolved, place the fixing solution into a 2 l glass storage bottle.

Methanol Fixing Solution

> 50 ml glacial acetic acid
> 450 ml methanol

Mix glacial acetic acid and methanol in a glass beaker and store in a glass or plastic storage bottle.

PROCESSING PROCEDURE

To fix or stabilize the blood on the surface of the evidence, thus preventing the blood print from running, use one of the following:

A) Immerse the article containing the impression in a glass tray of the Sulfosalicylic acid fixing solution for 5 min.
B) Spray or wash the surface with the methanol fixing solution.
C) Place the evidence in a laboratory oven set at 100 °C for 20 min.

SAFETY CONSIDERATIONS

A) Refer to MSDS for specified chemicals.
B) Follow proper safety precautions.
C) Use proper ventilation.
D) Wear suitable protective clothing, gloves, and goggles.
E) Avoid contact with skin and eyes.

LITERATURE REFERENCES

Boyd, Fred M., January 1990. Bloody Footwear Impression Enhanced by a Chemical Reaction. Florida Division of the International Association for Identification Newsletter, pp. 4–5.

Federal Bureau of Investigation. Chemical Formulas and Processing Guide for Developing Latent Prints, pp. 11–12, revised 1999.

Federal Bureau of Investigation. Use of Hazardous Substances in the Latent Fingerprint Laboratory, pp. 1–6.

Hamm, Ernest, 1983. Enhancement and development of blood prints. In: Paper Presented to the Georgia State Division of the International Association for Identification, pp. 1–12.

Coomassie Brilliant Blue R250

Category: Stain (reagent)
Reacts with: Blood protein
Process product: Blue–black colored stain where amido makes contact with blood protein
Color ██████████

PURPOSE

Coomassie Brilliant Blue R250 is used for the development or enhancement of latent prints, footwear, and tire impressions in suspected blood containing protein residue on porous and nonporous items.

MATERIALS

A) Coomassie Blue R250
B) Methanol
C) Glacial acetic acid
D) Distilled water
E) Scale, beakers, graduated cylinder, magnetic stirrer and stirring bar, and dark glass bottles for storage
F) Wash bottles, trays, and sprayers

MIXING PROCEDURE

Staining Solution

0.44 g Coomassie Blue
200 ml methanol
40 ml glacial acetic acid
200 ml distilled water

Add acid to the water first. Mix ingredients thoroughly using a magnetic stirrer (approximately 30 min). Store in a dark glass bottle.

Rinse Solution

40 ml glacial acetic acid
200 ml methanol
200 ml distilled water

Add acid to water first. Mix ingredients together; these can be mixed manually.

PROCESSING PROCEDURE

A) All visible prints or impressions of potential value in blood should be photographed prior to processing.

B) Prior to application, the suspected blood should be completely dry or fixed on the item to be processed.

C) Apply the developer to the specimen by dipping, spraying, or through the use of a chemical wash bottle.

D) Completely cover the target area until the desired development has been obtained.

E) Rinse the target area with the rinse solution to remove the background stain.

F) These steps can be repeated to improve the development and contrast.

G) After maximum clarity is achieved, apply the rinse solution again.

H) Allow the exhibit to air-dry.

I) All prints or impressions of potential value should be photographed.

SAFETY CONSIDERATIONS

A) Refer to MSDS for specified chemicals.

B) Use proper ventilation.

C) Avoid contact with skin or eyes.

D) Wear suitable protective clothing, gloves, and goggles.

E) Follow proper safety precautions.

LIMITATION

The use of Coomassie Blue R250 is limited to items that are contaminated with suspected blood.

QUALITY CONTROL

All reagent "working" solutions should be quality control tested at the time they are prepared. They should also be tested daily or prior to use on actual evidence. This quality control testing is to insure the accuracy of the mixture and that the desired reaction is being obtained.

LITERATURE REFERENCES

Federal Bureau of Investigation. Chemical Formulas and Processing Guide for Developing Latent Prints, pp. 49–50, revised 1999.

Norkus, P., Noppinger, K. New Reagent for the Enhancement of Blood Prints

Crowle's Double Stain

Category: Stain (reagent)
Reacts with: Blood protein
Process product: Blue–black colored stain where amido makes contact with blood protein
Color ███████████

PURPOSE

Crowle's Double Stain is used to develop or enhance latent prints, footwear, and tire impressions in suspected blood containing protein residue on nonporous surfaces.

MATERIALS

A) Crocein Scarlet 7B
B) Coomassie Brilliant Blue R
C) Glacial acetic acid
D) Trichloracetic acid
E) Distilled water
F) Scale, beakers, graduated cylinder, magnetic stirrer and stirring bar, and trays

MIXING PROCEDURE

Staining Solution

2.5 g Crocein Scarlet 7B
150 mg Coomassie Brilliant Blue R
50 ml glacial acetic acid
30 ml trichloracetic acid
1 l distilled water

The Crocein Scarlet 7B, Coomassie Brilliant Blue R, glacial acetic acid, and trichloracetic acid are combined and diluted into the distilled water. Place the solution on a magnetic stirring device until all the Crocein Scarlet 7B and Coomassie Brilliant Blue R are dissolved (approximately 30 min).

Rinse Solution

30 ml glacial acetic acid
970 ml distilled water

For safety, add the acid to the water. The rinse can be mixed manually

PROCESSING PROCEDURE

A) All visible prints or impressions of potential value in blood should be photographed prior to processing.

B) Prior to application, the suspected blood should be completely dry or fixed.

C) The evidence is placed in a tray or container with the staining solution and agitated.

D) Depending on the type of surface and age of the print, the prints or impressions will take 2–30 min to develop.

E) The evidence is then placed in the rinse solution for approximately 1 min and agitated until the background clears.

F) If more detail is required, the evidence can be restained numerous times.

G) All prints or impressions of potential value should be photographed.

SAFETY CONSIDERATIONS

A) Refer to MSDS for specified chemicals.

B) Use proper ventilation.

C) Avoid contact with skin or eyes.

D) Wear suitable protective clothing, gloves, and goggles.

E) Follow proper safety precautions.

LIMITATION

The use of Crowle's Double Stain is limited to items that are contaminated with suspected blood.

QUALITY CONTROL

All reagent "working" solutions should be quality control tested at the time they are prepared. They should also be tested daily or prior to use on actual evidence. This quality control testing is to insure the accuracy of the mixture and that the desired reaction is being obtained.

LITERATURE REFERENCES

Federal Bureau of Investigation. Chemical Formulas and Processing Guide for Developing Latent Prints, pp. 51–52, revised 1999.

Lee, Henry, C., Gaensslen, R.E., 1991. Advances in Fingerprint Technology, pp. 83–87.

Norkus, P., Noppinger, K. New Reagent for the Enhancement of Blood Prints

Crystal Violet

Category: Stain
Reacts with: Epithelial cells
Process product: Staining occurs when fingerprints on adhesive surfaces are dipped in crystal violet
Color ███████████

PURPOSE

Crystal violet (gentian violet) is a sensitive stain that reacts with epithelial cells and other proteins of latent print residue transferred upon surface contact. Crystal violet is usually very effective on surfaces that readily hold the deposited sebum, such as the adhesive side of tape.

MATERIALS

A) Crystal violet
B) Distilled water
C) Ethyl alcohol (method 2)
D) Hydrochloric acid (method 2)
E) Scale, graduated cylinder, magnetic stirrer and stir bar, and a dark colored glass bottle
F) Wash bottles and trays
G) Tap water
H) Photo-Flo and photographic paper

MIXING PROCEDURE METHOD 1

0.1 g crystal violet
100 ml distilled water

Combine the ingredients and stir on a magnetic stirring device for approximately 25 min.

MIXING PROCEDURE METHOD 2

Stock solution: Mix 1.5 g crystal violet in 100 ml ethyl alcohol.
Working solution: Dilute 2 ml of the crystal violet stock solution in 100 ml of tap water.
Clearing solution: To 90 ml of tap water, add 10 ml of hydrochloric acid.

Never add the water to the acid.

PROCESSING PROCEDURE

A) Apply the crystal violet by dipping, spraying, or through the use of a chemical wash bottle.

B) Leave the item in the solution and agitate gently until the desired development has been reached.

C) Rinse the item gently with tap water.

D) If the desired development or contrast was not obtained, the solution can be reapplied.

E) Rinse again.

F) The item can be examined with normal lighting or with a forensic light source. The suggested excitation wavelengths would be 525, 530, and 570 nm and viewed through red goggles. If using 485 or 450 nm, try using orange goggles.

G) All prints of potential value should be photographed.

H) Dark colored tapes may not present sufficient contrast to permit photographic recording of the impression. A transfer of the stained impression is possible by immersing the processed tape in a standard Photo-Flo solution and placing the impression side on a sheet of unexposed, fixed, washed and dried, resin-coated photographic paper. F surface RC papers accept the transfer better than N surface. All excess water is gently removed with absorbent tissue, and the two items are firmly pressed together for 10 min. After pressing, the tape is slowly peeled from the photographic paper.

SAFETY CONSIDERATIONS

A) Refer to MSDS for specified chemicals.

B) Wear suitable protective clothing and gloves.

C) Follow proper safety precautions.

LIMITATION

Crystal violet works primarily on the adhesive surfaces, but this does not preclude other applications.

QUALITY CONTROL

All reagent "working" solutions should be quality control tested at the time they are prepared. They should also be tested daily or prior to use on actual evidence. This quality control testing is to insure the accuracy of the mixture and that the desired reaction is being obtained.

LITERATURE REFERENCES

Federal Bureau of Investigation. Chemical Formulas and Processing Guide for Developing Latent Prints, p. 25, revised 1999.

Lee, Henry, C., Gaensslen, R.E., 1991. Advances in Fingerprint Technology, pp. 83–87.

Technical Note on Crystal Violet. Lightning Powder Company, Inc., pp. 1–4.

Truszkowski, G., Laninga, K., February 1984. A Modified Approach in Development of Latent Prints on Black Plastic Using Crystal Violet Dye and Photographic Paper. Identification News, p. 2.

Wilson, Benjamin L., McCloud, Vernon D., March 1982. Development of Latent Prints on Black Plastic Tape Using Crystal Violet Dye and Photographic Paper. Identification News, pp. 3–4.

Cyanoacrylate Fuming (CA)
Category: Physical
Reacts with: Fingerprint matrix
Process product: White powdery residue
Color [ ]

PURPOSE

Cyanoacrylate esters are the active ingredients in the super bond adhesives and are generally available according to the type of alcohols used in manufacturing. Most cyanoacrylates are methyl or ethyl esters. Regardless of type, the esters volatize into chain molecules with a positive electrical charge. In an atmosphere of relatively high humidity, the cyanoacrylate ester molecules are attracted to fingerprint residue and polymerize upon the deposit. The exact nature of the polymerization is not yet understood, but certain consequences do affect the latent print processing procedures.

Cyanoacrylate ester fuming is highly effective with nonporous items made of plastic or metal. It is superior for the processing of gun metal. Glass or sealed wood surfaces reflect marginally better with cyanoacrylate ester fuming than with powder or particulate processing as an initial examination technique, but they provide considerably improved results with luminescent dye stain or small particulate reagent secondary processing. Use of cyanoacrylate fuming with porous items sometimes inhibits or diminishes more successful chemical techniques.

The cyanoacrylate fuming procedure may be timed with the use of test prints. Microscope slides are convenient test items when deliberately deposited with a test impression and placed near the item(s). Processing should be terminated when the test impressions have reached optimum development. Nickel and chrome items, however, should be watched carefully, as faster development may occur. Conversely, vinyl, rubber, and leather items may require additional processing time. Excessive exposure of surfaces to a high concentration of fumes can result in overdevelopment, which may obscure ridge formation due to total surface polymerization.

MATERIALS

A) Super bond adhesive containing cyanoacrylate ester (liquid compound or pouch)
B) Tank, plastic enclosure, or fuming cabinet
C) Container of lukewarm water
D) Chemical heat source (sodium hydroxide and absorbent cotton)
E) Electrical heat source (cup warmer or light bulb)
F) Aluminum weigh boat or watch glass

Note: Not all materials will be needed in all instances. Refer to procedures for exact uses.

PROCESSING PROCEDURE

Vapors must be contained and a tank or plastic enclosure can be used. However, a fuming cabinet is most often used. Volatilization of cyanoacrylate ester at normal room temperature is relatively slow but is a viable procedure for processing. Polymerization may be retarded or prevented by low humidity. The addition of a container of lukewarm water usually will improve fuming results. However, items must not be placed closer than three inches to the water.

Development time at room temperature may require several hours or even days in large capacity containers.

Application of heat greatly accelerates volatilization. Cyanoacrylate ester reacts with bases and a **celluloid catalyst** to produce extremely rapid volatilization with the generation of chemical heat. A 0.5 normal solution of sodium hydroxide is used to saturate a roll of absorbent cotton, and the roll is dried. Small squares can be cut from the roll. The square pad is placed in the fuming enclosure and the adhesive applied directly to the cotton pad. Reaction is immediate in the form of white, acid vapors. The container must be sealed quickly and eye or nasal contact with the vapors should be avoided. Polymerization is usually complete after 10–15 min. However, factors such as volume, cotton saturation, and speed of closure may alter development time considerably.

One alternative, which offers rapid development time with a minimum health risk, is to use a **light bulb** as the heat source. A standard light receptacle is added to the processing tank with a wire loop support fashioned to hold a watch glass approximately 1 inch above the light bulb. The adhesive is dropped on the watch glass with the light out. Once the container is covered, the light is turned on. Rapid volatilization does not begin until the heat of the bulb penetrates the watch glass, but once started, is complete. Natural convection currents aid dispersal of the fumes, and development is usually accomplished in about 15 min. The light should be extinguished at the first sight of polymerization.

A second alternative, which also offers rapid development time with a minimum health risk, is to use a **cup warmer** as the heat source. A cup warmer can be added to the processing tank along with a small container, such as an aluminum weigh boat. A few drops of adhesive are then placed into the aluminum weigh boat. The cabinet or tank must be closed before, or immediately after, turning on the cup warmer. Rapid volatilization does not begin until the adhesive is heated. Natural convection currents aid dispersal of the fumes, and development is usually accomplished in about 15 min. The cup warmer should be turned off at the first sight of polymerization.

A very convenient and effective method is the use of a product such as Loctite Hard Evidence® pouches. Cyanoacrylate esters are mixed in a gel with chemicals that produce fairly rapid but controlled volatilization upon exposure to air. The product is available in pouches, which are easily peeled open to commence the volatilization but can be resealed to stop the reaction. Each pouch will produce fumes for 10 to 15 h depending upon ambient temperature. However, volatilization slows with exposure so that more time must be allowed for pouches approaching exhaustion. A pouch with less than 5 h of usage generally will require 40 min for optimum polymerization in a 10-gallon volume. Processing time may be halved by the use of a second pouch.

Pouches anticipated to be stored for longer than six months should be refrigerated, but not frozen, and allowed to reach room temperature before use. However, previously opened pouches should not be refrigerated. Opened pouches, which may not be used again for some time, should be sealed with tape to prevent the gradual release of fumes. Vinyl or electrical tapes are recommended.

RESULTS

Photographic preservation of all suitable polymerized impressions is recommended prior to any additional processing. Once the latent impressions are recorded, further processing sometimes reveals impressions in which polymerization was too indistinct for visual notice or did not occur. Powders and particulate developers are effective and often permit additional photographic and lifting preservation. Small Particulate Reagent (SPR) will sometimes adhere to faint impressions when powder will not. Luminescent dye application is generally effective after powder, particulate, or SPR application, as the liquid dye solution will normally wash away the particle remnants. However, vinyl, rubber, oily guns, and hard plastic, especially those used in cash register drawers, may not be receptive to any powder or particulate method.

SAFETY CONSIDERATIONS

A) Cyanoacrylate fumes can irritate eyes and nasal passages. Exposure to fumes should be avoided.
B) Contact of the skin with cyanoacrylate ester liquid should be avoided.
C) Refer to MSDS for additional information.
D) Follow proper safety precautions.

LIMITATIONS

Cyanoacrylate fuming is limited in use to nonporous items or semiporous items that have a shiny or coated finish, such as the cover of a telephone book.

Properties of the polymer are dependent upon the type of cyanoacrylate ester used. Both ethyl and methyl esters produce a white coating. Ethyl ester polymers are softer and less durable, while methyl esters can usually only be removed with solvents. However, the durable, hard property of the methyl ester may inhibit dye applications, especially with Rhodamine 6G. Any product containing ethyl ester generally will be more effective when subsequent luminescent dye applications are indicated.

QUALITY CONTROL

Cyanoacrylate ester liquid should be quality control tested daily or prior to use on actual evidence. This quality control testing is to insure the desired reaction is being obtained.

LITERATURE REFERENCES

U. S. Department of Justice, Federal Bureau of Investigation, Laboratory Division, 2000. Processing Guide for Developing Latent Prints.

Florida Department of Law Enforcement, Latent Print Analyst Training Program, Task VII-Chemical Processing.

Technical Notes, Chemical Processing for Latent Prints. Lighting Powder Company, 1998.

DAB (Diaminobenzidine)

Category: Reagent
Reacts with: Heme groups in hemoglobin (blood)
Process product: DAB oxidizes to a brown color when in contact with heme
Color ■■■■■■■■

PURPOSE

DAB (Diaminobenzidine) is used for the development or enhancement of bloody latent prints, footwear, and tire impressions. DAB is particularly effective on old blood prints.

MATERIALS

A) 5-Sulphosalicylic Acid
B) Distilled water
C) 1 M phosphate buffer (pH 7.4)
D) DAB
E) Hydrogen peroxide
F) Graduated cylinders, scale, beakers, magnetic stirrer and stirring bar, and storage bottles
G) Four trays (designated for the four steps)
H) Three chemical wash bottles or sprayers (designated for three separate solutions)
I) Tissues (nonperfumed)
J) Hair dryer

MIXING PROCEDURE

Solution A (Fixer)

20 g 5-Sulphosalicylic Acid
1 l distilled water
Dissolve 5-Sulphosalicylic Acid in distilled water. Store in a dark bottle at room temperature.

Solution B (Buffer)

100 ml 1 M phosphate buffer (pH of 7.4)
800 ml distilled water
Mix 1 M phosphate buffer with distilled water. Store at room temperature.

Solution C (DAB)

1 g 3, 3′-Diamino-benzidinetetrahydrochloride
100 ml distilled water

Thoroughly mix; care should be taken that the ingredients are thoroughly dissolved.

Solution D (Developer)

180 ml solution B
20 ml solution C
1 ml hydrogen peroxide 30%
Thoroughly mix.

PROCESSING PROCEDURE

All prints or impressions of potential value in blood should be photographed prior to processing.

Submersion Method

This method consists of four (4) dipping steps using four (4) trays, each containing one (1) solution A through D, followed by steps E and F

A) Fixer solution: Submerge the specimen in this solution for approximately 3–5 min.
B) Distilled water: Submerge the specimen in distilled water for 30 s to 1 min to rinse the specimen.
C) Developer solution: Submerge the specimen for 5 min for maximum development. The specimen may be removed prior to 5 min if maximum development or contrast has been achieved.
D) Distilled water: Submerge the specimen in distilled water to stop the developer solution from overdeveloping the prints.
E) The specimen can be air-dried or dried with heat, such as with a hair dryer.
F) All prints or impressions of potential value should be photographed.

Tissue/Paper Towel Method

This method applies to solutions by squirt bottles or a spray apparatus onto a tissue paper towel that has been placed over the area to be processed. The tissues used for this process must be durable enough to be placed and picked up while wet, without totally disintegrating. Perfumed tissues should not be used, as the chemicals contained therein can interfere with the development process. Unscented white facial or hand tissues and thin paper towels are acceptable.

A) Fixer: Using a chemical wash bottle with fixer solution, squirt this solution onto a tissue that has been placed on the area to be examined. The tissue adheres to the area because it is wet from the fixer. This tissue should be kept wet for 3–5 min.

B) Distilled water: Remove the tissue. Using a chemical wash bottle with distilled water, squirt the water on the processed area for 30 s to 1 min.

C) Developer: Place a new tissue on the area to be processed. After the new tissue is in place, the developer solution is squirted onto the tissue using a chemical wash bottle. The tissue must be kept wet at all times and maintained on the area for 5 min. As with the submersion method, this time period may be less if maximum development or contrast has been achieved.

D) Distilled water: Remove the tissue. Using a chemical wash bottle with distilled water, squirt the water on the processed area for 30 s to 1 min.

E) The specimen can be air-dried or dried with heat, such as with a hair dryer.

F) All prints or impressions of potential value should be photographed.

SAFETY CONSIDERATIONS

A) Refer to MSDS for specified chemicals.
B) Use proper ventilation.
C) Avoid contact with skin and eyes.
D) Wear suitable protective clothing, gloves, and goggles.
E) Follow proper safety precautions.

LIMITATIONS

A) The use of DAB is limited to items that are contaminated with suspected blood.
B) DAB must be done before the Amido Black process, but it has no effect on subsequent processing by Amido Black.
C) Ninhydrin has no effect on the DAB process.
D) Cyanoacrylate fuming has an adverse effect on the DAB process.

QUALITY CONTROL

All reagent "working" solutions should be quality control tested at the time they are prepared. They should also be tested daily or prior to use on actual evidence. This quality control testing is to insure the accuracy of the mixture and that the desired reaction is being obtained.

LITERATURE REFERENCE

Federal Bureau of Investigation. Chemical Formulas and Processing Guide for Developing Latent Prints, pp. 18–20.

DFO (1,8-Diazafluoren-9-one)

Category: Reagent
Reacts with: Amino acid
Process product: Fluorescent yellow when it reacts with amino acids

Color [   ]

PURPOSE

DFO (1,8-Diazafluoren-9-one) is a Ninhydrin analogue that reacts to the amino acids present in the body protein.

MATERIALS

A) DFO
B) Methanol
C) Ethyl acetate
D) Acetic acid
E) Propanol
F) Acetone
G) Xylene
H) Petroleum ether
I) Scale, graduated cylinders, beakers, trays, magnetic stirrer and stirring bar, and dark storage bottles
J) Forensic light source
K) Oven, hair dryer, or iron

MIXING PROCEDURES

Stock Solution

0.5 g DFO
100 ml methanol
100 ml ethyl acetate
20 ml acetic acid

Working Solution

60 ml DFO stock solution
10 ml propanol
50 ml acetone
50 ml xylene
830 ml petroleum ether

Do not mix the working solution until you are ready to use it. It is recommended to mix only enough working solution that will be used within 2–3 weeks.

PROCESSING PROCEDURE

A) The item should be dipped into the working solution for 10 s and allowed to dry for about 3 min.

B) Step A should be repeated, as dipping and drying twice seems to be better than one application.

C) Heat is then applied through the use of an oven. The item should be heated for 20 min at approximately 100 °C (212 °F). A hair dryer, photo mounting press, or dry iron can also be used.

D) Most plastic will tolerate a temperature of 50 °C, but samples of articles should be tested if possible to determine the maximum temperature to which they can be subjected without damage. At lower temperatures, it is advisable to heat for longer periods of time, possibly several hours.

E) View the item under a forensic light source. Wavelengths with the orange goggles are 450, 485, 525, and 530 nm for most papers. Manila envelopes, brown paper bags, cardboard, craft paper, and most yellow legal pad paper should be viewed at 570–590 nm through a red filter.

F) All prints of potential value should be photographed.

Note: When DFO is being used as a blood print developer, the blood should be "fixed" prior to processing.

SAFETY CONSIDERATIONS

A) Refer to MSDS for specified chemicals.

B) Follow proper safety precautions.

C) Use in a fume hood.

D) Wear suitable protective clothing, gloves, and goggles.

E) Avoid contact with skin and eyes.

F) When examining the evidence with a light source, wear protective goggles.

LIMITATIONS

A) DFO must be visualized with a forensic light source.

B) When DFO, Ninhydrin, and physical developer are to be used in processing the item, DFO must be used as the first process.

QUALITY CONTROL

All reagent "working" solutions should be quality control tested at the time they are prepared. They should also be tested daily or prior to use on actual evidence. This quality control testing is to insure the accuracy of the mixture and that the desired reaction is being obtained.

LITERATURE REFERENCES

Federal Bureau of Investigation. Chemical Formulas and Processing Guide for Developing Latent Prints, pp. 21–22, revised 1999.

Home Office Police Scientific Development Branch, 1990. Fingerprint Detection by Fluorescence Examination, p. 30.

Technical Note on DFO. Lightning Powder Company, Inc., pp. 1–5.

Menzel, E. Roland, 1991. An Introduction to Lasers, Forensic Lights and Fluorescent Fingerprint Detection Techniques, pp. 42–44.

DYE STAINS

- Dye stains bind to cyanoacrylate that has polymerized to fingerprint residue. The dye stains are made visible by exposure to light produced by a forensic light source. Different dye stains require different wavelengths (color) of light to fluoresce.
- Dye stains are applied by dipping, washing, or spraying (in fume hood).
- Dye staining does not preclude the use of powders. In fact, CA processed fingerprints can be powdered and lifted numerous times.

The following is a short list of available dye stains:

Dye Stain	Light Wavelength
Ardrox	300–450 nm
Basic red	450 nm
Basic yellow	300–450 nm
MBD	450 nm
M-Star	450 nm
Rhodamine 6G	450–480 nm
RAM (Rhodamine, Ardrox, MBD mixture)	300–480 nm
Safranin-O	450 nm
TEC	365 nm longwave UV

> **Fluorescein**
>
> Category: Stain (reagent)
> Reacts with: Blood protein
> Process product: Fluorescent yellow-colored stain where contact is made with blood protein
> Color [   ]

PURPOSE

Fluorescein is a two-step chemical process that causes a reaction to occur between the hemoglobin in blood and oxygen. This reaction causes a fluorescent product that can be visualized under a forensic light source.

MATERIALS

A) Commercially available fluorescein solutions A, B, and C
B) Two sprayers
C) Forceps
D) Forensic light source, such as a CrimeScope or ultraviolet lights
E) Goggles

MIXING PROCEDURE

Fluorescein is a commercially prepared chemical and should be mixed per the directions of the particular manufacture specifications.

PROCESSING PROCEDURE

A) All visible prints or impressions of potential value in blood should be photographed prior to processing.
B) Prior to application, the suspected blood should be completely dry or fixed on the item to be processed.
C) Lightly spray the item with mixed fluorescein reagents part A and part B— DO NOT OVERSPRAY.
D) Allow the area to dry completely.
E) Respray with fluorescein reagent part C.
F) Allow the area to dry thoroughly.
G) View at 415 nm through 535 nm wavelengths with a forensic light source or UV light.
H) Visualization of the reaction is best within 10–15 min after drying.
I) All prints or impressions of potential value should be photographed.

SAFETY CONSIDERATIONS

A) Refer to MSDS for specified chemicals.
B) Use proper ventilation.

C) Avoid contact with skin and eyes.

D) Wear suitable protective clothing, gloves, and goggles.

E) The use of a respirator is recommended in the MSDS, as well as the instruction sheet for fluorescein.

F) Follow proper safety precautions.

LIMITATION

The use of fluorescein is limited to items that are contaminated with suspected blood.

QUALITY CONTROL

All reagent "working" solutions should be quality control tested at the time they are prepared. They should also be tested daily or prior to use on actual evidence. This quality control testing is to insure the accuracy of the mixture and that the desired reaction is being obtained.

SHELF LIFE/STORAGE

The mixed fluorescein reagents A and B have a usable shelf life of 2–3 h. The unmixed fluorescein reagents have a shelf life of approximately four months if stored at room temperature. The shelf life has not been determined but is much longer if stored in the refrigerator.

LITERATURE REFERENCES

Cheeseman, Rob, Allyn DiMeo, L. Fluorescein as a Field Worthy Latent Bloodstain Detection System. http://www.arcanaforensics.com/fluorescein. html.

DeHaan, J.D., Clark, J.D., Spear, T.F., Oswalt, R., Barney, S.S. Chemical Enhancement of Fingerprints in Blood: An Evaluation of Methods, Effects on DNA, and Assessment of Chemical Hazards. http://www.latent-prints.com/cac_bllod.htm.

Fluorescein. Crime Scene Supply, Inc.

Fluorescent Dye Pink
Category: Dye stain
Reacts with: Bonds to cyanoacrylate residue
Process product: Fluorescent pink stain adheres to CA residue that has polymerized
to fingerprint matrix
Color

PURPOSE

Fluorescent Dye Pink is a water tracing dye that is readily absorbed by cyanoacrylate-developed impressions and should luminesce when exposed to a forensic light source.

MATERIALS

A) Fluorescent Dye Pink
B) Methanol
C) Scale, graduated cylinder, trays, wash bottles, mixing device, and sprayers
D) Storage containers
E) Hair dryer
F) Forensic light source

MIXING PROCEDURE

0.5 g Fluorescent Dye Pink
100 ml methanol

Solution easily mixes in a storage container.

PROCESSING PROCEDURE

A) Fume evidence with cyanoacrylate.
Examples:
Plastic bags
Glass
Most metal surfaces
Wood
Glossy papers
B) Dip, pour, or spray over surface.
C) Dry thoroughly; a hair dryer may be used to accelerate drying.
D) Examine under a forensic light source to include wavelengths in the ultraviolet region.
E) Photograph usable latent prints.

F) In some instances, the fluorescent dye may be absorbed by contaminants or excess cyanoacrylate deposits on the surface and may tend to obscure the impressions. A rinse with methanol will, in most cases, remove the background dye without damaging the impression. If, however, the dye in the impression is washed away by the methanol, the print can be easily restained without any loss of detail in most cases.

G) Fluorescent Dye Pink does not interfere with subsequent powdering and lifting of the impressions.

H) All prints of potential value should be photographed.

SAFETY CONSIDERATIONS

A) Refer to MSDS for specified chemicals.

B) Use in fume hood.

C) Use of high-quality, liquid-repellent gloves, and even double gloving is recommended.

D) Fluorescent Dye Pink is not listed as a carcinogen; the MSDS lists that it has been known to cause cancer in laboratory rats.

E) Due to possible health risks, only the necessary amount for processing should be prepared at one time. Remaining amounts of the Dye Pink solution should be stored in a sealed container and disposed of in the proper manner for hazardous chemicals.

F) Follow proper safety precautions.

LIMITATION

The use of Fluorescent Dye Pink is limited to nonporous surfaces that have been previously processed with cyanoacrylate.

QUALITY CONTROL

All reagent "working" solutions should be quality control tested at the time they are prepared. They should also be tested daily or prior to use on actual evidence. This quality control testing is to insure the accuracy of the mixture and that the desired reaction is being obtained.

LITERATURE REFERENCE

Olsen, Robert D. A Practical Fluorescent Dye Staining Technique for Cyanoacrylate-Developed Latent Prints.

Forensic Light Sources
Category: Physical
Reacts with: Photoluminescent materials
Process product: Visualize fingerprints through fluorescence
Color Visible spectrum

PURPOSE

The development of the forensic light source is actually the development of the science of luminescence as applied to the detection of physical evidence, particularly latent prints. When used in combination with cyanoacrylate fuming, luminescent dye stains, and powder, forensic light sources can prove to be a very valuable tool. Other types of evidence that may be detected through the use of a forensic light source include footwear and tire impressions. Many forensic light sources have the capabilities of producing various wavelengths of light, including ultraviolet and infrared. These light sources are available from a number of manufacturers.

MATERIALS

A) Forensic light source(s), such as:
B) CrimeScope CS16
C) Mini CrimeScope
D) Luma-Lite
E) Polilight
F) Omnichrome
G) Shortwave ultraviolet light
H) Longwave ultraviolet light

PROCEDURES

Specific procedures for each and every available forensic light source cannot be outlined in this document. It is best to read and periodically review the operation/instruction manuals that are supplied with the equipment by the manufacturer.

SAFETY CONSIDERATIONS

The eyes and the skin are the most susceptible areas when using forensic light sources. Goggles should be worn to protect the eyes. When using ultraviolet light, particularly shortwave, a full-face shield may be warranted. Refer to the manufacturer's recommended safety procedures.

LIMITATION

Not suitable for use on surfaces that may be damaged by heat generated or by high-intensity illuminations.

QUALITY CONTROL

All forensic light sources should be properly maintained for optimum performance. Anyone operating the forensic light source should be familiar with the specific operation of the equipment as specified by the manufacturer's operation manual or instructions.

LITERATURE REFERENCES

Creer, K., May 24–28, 1993. Detection and Photography of Latent Prints Using Ultraviolet Radiation and Other Light Sources. In: International Symposium on the Forensic Aspects of Latent Prints. FBI Academy.

Fischer, J.F., May 24–28, 1993. Forensic Light Sources and Their Use in Conjunction with Luminescent Techniques. In: International Symposium on the Forensic Aspects of Latent Prints. FBI Academy.

Florida Department of Law Enforcement. Latent Print Training Manual, Chapter 8, Latent Print Development with Specialized Light Sources.

Heat/Flame Particulates

Category: Physical
Reacts with: Fingerprint residue
Process product: Soot
Color ███████ or [   ]

PURPOSE

Conditions similar to the particulate developer procedure, which deliberately uses fine particle soot to develop latent impressions by igniting camphor or other resinous materials, may occur during the early stages of a fire. The criminal investigation of an arson may discover a nonporous container of heat-resistant material used to transport the suspected accelerant or to serve as the origin of the flame. In areas of relative confinement, the initial stages of the fire may produce sufficient fine particles, which interact with latent print residue before destruction of the deposit can occur. Subsequent build-up of soot over the latent impression may form protective layers that seal and harden the particulate impregnated residues. The exact combination of conditions is unknown, but metal containers and glass articles severely charred and seemingly heat-destroyed may yield suitable latent prints. This procedure, based upon methods devised by the Houston Fire Department, appears to be more effective with items exposed to high heat levels rather than those in which the fire was extinguished in early stages. Regardless of conditions, charred items from an arson investigation should be examined for latent print evidence.

MATERIALS

A) Fiberglass brush
B) Stiff brush or coarse cloth
C) Water
D) Paper towels
E) Commercial dryer
F) Lifting tape

Note: All materials may not be used. Condition of the evidence will dictate the use of materials. Refer to procedures for proper use.

PROCEDURES

Initial examination of items blackened from exposure to fire is made to determine the condition of the soot deposit. Lightly-coated items or those with readily-flaking soot deposits should be processed with a brush. This merely duplicates the particulate method by removing excessive soot to reveal any developed prints.

Items with heavy charring exhibited by hardened layers of sooty deposit are processed by placing them beneath a moderate to high flow of cold water. While beneath the stream of water, the articles are scrubbed with a stiff brush or rubbed with a coarse cloth to remove as much loosened sooty deposit as possible. Considerable pressure may be applied during this process, as long as the actual prying of the layers is avoided. When all loosened soot is removed, the items are dried with towels or forced air. A section of lifting tape is then applied to an area and pressed firmly onto the charred material and removed. This procedure is repeated until the surface becomes exposed. If conditions during the early stage of the fire have been favorable, latent impressions impregnated by the soot will be bonded to the surface and will be revealed. Light contact to the impression area with lifting tape may aid removing any remaining sooty flakes.

RESULTS

Exposed bonded impressions are highly resistant to damage and will remain on the surface without the need for protection. Normally bonded impressions cannot be lifted successfully and must be photographically preserved.

SAFETY CONSIDERATIONS

A) The fine particle soot should not be inhaled and examination should be conducted in a well-ventilated area or fume hood.

B) Follow proper safety precautions.

LIMITATION

This technique is limited to nonporous items of heat-resistant material.

QUALITY CONTROL

This method relies on the removal, rather than the application, of fine particles deposited on an item of evidence during a fire. Therefore, the particulate cannot be control tested.

LITERATURE REFERENCE

Carol Herring, April–June 1992. This May "Soot" Your Arson Cases. F.D.I.A.I. News, p. 3.

IND (1,2 indanedione)

Category: Reagent
Reacts with: Amino acid
Process product: Fluorescent yellow when it reacts with amino acids

Color [   ]

PURPOSE

IND (1,2 indanedione) is a chemical that reacts to the amino acids present in the body protein to produce fluorescent detail on porous items when exposed to a forensic light source.

MATERIALS

A) 1,2 indanedione
B) Ethyl acetate
C) HFE 7100 (3M corporation product)
D) Scale, graduated cylinders, beakers, trays, magnetic stirrer and stirring bar, and dark storage bottles
E) Forensic light source
F) Oven, hair dryer, or iron

MIXING PROCEDURE

Working Solution

2 g 1,2 indanedione
70 ml ethyl acetate
930 ml HFE 7100
Dissolve 2 g of 1,2 indanedione in 70 ml of ethyl acetate. Add enough HFE 7100 to make a final volume of 1 l.

PROCESSING PROCEDURE

A) The item should be dipped, sprayed, or washed with the IND solution and allowed to dry for about 3 min.
B) Heat is then applied through the use of an oven, photo mounting press, hair dryer, or dry iron. The item should be oven heated for 20 min at approximately 100 °C (212 °F). Mounting press times are considerably less, 2–5 min at 100 °C.
C) Most plastic will tolerate a temperature of 50 °C, but samples of articles should be tested if possible to determine the maximum temperature to which they can be subjected without damage. At lower temperatures, it is advisable to heat for longer periods of time, possibly several hours.

D) View the item under a forensic light source. Wavelengths with the orange goggles are 450, 485, 515, and 530 nm. For most papers, 515 nm appears to be the optimum wavelength. Manila envelopes, brown paper bags, cardboard, craft paper, and most yellow legal pad paper should be viewed at 515–570 nm through an orange or red filter.

E) All prints of potential value should be photographed.

SAFETY CONSIDERATIONS

A) Refer to MSDS for specified chemicals.

B) Follow proper safety precautions.

C) Use in a fume hood.

D) Wear suitable protective clothing, gloves, and goggles.

E) Avoid contact with skin and eyes.

F) When examining the evidence with a light source, wear protective goggles.

LIMITATIONS

A) IND should be visualized with a forensic light source for best results.

B) When IND and Ninhydrin are to be used in processing the item, IND should be used as the first process. Fingerprints that have been developed by Ninhydrin can be further enhanced by processing with IND but may not fluoresce.

QUALITY CONTROL

All reagent "working" solutions should be quality control tested at the time they are prepared. They should also be tested daily or prior to use on actual evidence. This quality control testing is to insure the accuracy of the mixture and that the desired reaction is being obtained.

LITERATURE REFERENCES

Almog, J., Springer, E., Wiesner, S., Frank, A., Khodzhaev, O., Lidor, R., Varkony, H., Dayan, S., 1999. Latent fingerprint visualization by 1,2 indanedione and related compounds: preliminary results. Journal of Forensic Sciences 44 (1), 114–118.

Wiesner, S., Springer, E., Sasson, Y., Almog, J., 2001. Chemical development of latent fingerprints: 1,2 indanedione has come of age. Journal of Forensic Sciences 46 (5), 1082–1084.

Home Office Police Scientific Development Branch, 1990. Fingerprint Detection by Fluorescence Examination, p. 30.

Menzel, E. Roland, 1991. An Introduction to Lasers, Forensic Lights and Fluorescent Fingerprint Detection Techniques, pp. 42–44.

Modifications to the 1,2 Indanedione Process
1,2 indanedione-zinc
0.08% IND-Zn (with ethyl acetate)

MATERIALS

0.08% w/v IND-Zn ethyl acetate formulation:

A) 0.8 g 1,2 indanedione
B) 90 ml ethyl acetate 10 ml acetic acid (glacial)
C) 80 ml zinc chloride (stock)*
D) 820 ml petroleum ether

*zinc chloride stock:

A) 0.4 g zinc chloride
B) 10 ml absolute ethanol
C) 1 ml ethyl acetate
D) 190 ml petroleum ether

MIXING PROCEDURE

Combine ingredients and stir on a stirring device for approximately 20 min, until the 1,2 indanedione is dissolved.

Make sure bottle is thoroughly cleaned and free of excess moisture with a final methanol wash (triple rinse).

The glassware must be very clean. If not properly cleaned, the solution will be cloudy. While this typically goes away in 24 h, it was found during research that sometimes it can cause the chemicals to fall out of the solution.

0.08% IND-Zn with ethyl acetate produces a brighter fluorescence and often additional detail when compared to DFO HFE71DE.

Processing Procedure
Safety Considerations
Limitations
Quality Control
Same as above.

LITERATURE REFERENCES

Stoilovic, M., Lennard, C., Wallace-Kunkel, C., Roux, C., 2007. Evaluation of a 1,2- indanedione formulation containing zinc chloride for improved fingermark detection on paper. Journal of Forensics Identification 57 (1).

Bicknell, Danna E., Ramotowski, Robert S., September 2008. Use of an optimized 1,2-indanedione process. Journal of Forensic Science 53 (5).

Iodine Fuming
Category: Physical
Reacts with: Lipids
Process product: Temporary discoloration
Color █████████
Procedures
Iodine fuming cabinet
Iodine fuming box and pad—"shake and bake"
Iodine fuming gun

PURPOSE

Iodine is a sensitive indicator of various fatty oils, which are often present in latent print residue. While palmer perspiration contains no oils, the mobility of the hands creates contact with other areas of the body where sebaceous glands are located, and oils are transferred to the friction ridge skin to become part of subsequent contact deposits.

Iodine is absorbed by the oily material, which assumes a reddish-brown color. While absorption is quite rapid and can be most pronounced, no chemical change occurs to either substance. When exposure to the iodine ceases, the oily material releases the iodine molecules slowly. The color begins to fade and after several hours, the iodine may be completely dissipated. Return exposure will most often repeat the process, while retained exposure prevents dissipation. Generally, iodine dissipates with no trace of exposure or damage to the article.

MATERIALS

A) Iodine crystals
B) Fuming cabinet, fuming box, fuming pad, plastic bag, or fuming gun
C) Calcium chloride (for use with fuming gun)
D) Glass wool (for use with fuming gun)

PROCEDURES

Iodine is most effectively utilized with vapors from heated crystals. Direct contact of iodine crystals to actual items should be avoided. Heat accelerates the action, and confined vapors provide for the best reaction and the least health risk.

Iodine Fuming Cabinet

Cabinets that permit adequate space for evidentiary items, fume containment, and gentle heat to accelerate sublimation are sometimes used. While there are commercially available cabinets, one can be easily constructed of wood and glass, which is even more effective and is less susceptible to the corrosive nature of vapors.

Iodine fuming cabinets, once a staple of latent print processing areas, have practically disappeared in most laboratories. The ineffectiveness of iodine vapor to visualize impressions more than 10 days after deposit and the effectiveness of Ninhydrin to develop older latent impressions resulted in an almost total abandonment of iodine fuming. However, with the discovery of 7,8-benzoflavone enhancement of iodine-visualized impressions and the very low destructive potential of iodine, iodine fuming cabinets may be considered as a viable addition to latent print processing equipment.

Commercially manufactured cabinets are available that use an electric heater to speed the iodine crystal sublimation. These cabinets work well but have two drawbacks, which can limit their operational life. First, the top lid is hinged and does not fit snugly. Vapors can escape unless a weight is used. The plastic hinges are not corroded by the iodine vapors but will break after heavy usage. Second, the cabinet is constructed of vinyl-coated metal. Any scratch or removal of the vinyl exposes the metal to iodine vapors that will eventually destroy the cabinet.

An iodine fuming cabinet can be constructed using wood and glass, which will function well without danger of corrosion. A diagram is included in the appendix that provides the general construction guidelines. Modifications may be preferred, especially in the heat source and baseboard, to avoid safety and health risks. An electric bulb can be used in lieu of the alcohol burner, which removes the need for asbestos. The essential design features are a sealed chamber with a well-fitting lid, at least one glass viewing window, and supports for a moveable device to hold items suspended in the vapor atmosphere.

Iodine Fuming Box and Pad—"Shake and Bake" (Plastic Bag)

A very simple yet effective means of iodine fuming involves the creation of temporary enclosures, referred to as a fuming box, pad, or bag. The use of a plastic bag involves a small amount of iodine crystals being poured into a bag, the item inserted, and the bag sealed. The crystals are held between the fingers or grabbed by the hand to provide additional heat to hasten vaporization. The bag may be periodically shaken to improve the distribution of the iodine vapors, but contact of the item with the loose crystals should be avoided. Oily impressions will discolor in a matter of minutes. The iodine fuming box can be assembled using any shallow box or tray. Two pieces of blotting paper are cut to fit the box or tray. One piece of blotting paper is placed on the bottom of the box or tray, iodine crystals are sprinkled evenly over it, and they are covered with the second piece of blotting paper. The item for examination is put on the top, and the enclosure is sealed with a glass cover. Sublimation will occur slowly at room temperature or is hastened by placing the fuming box beneath a flood lamp.

The fuming pad can be utilized to process larger areas or items that, although flat, will not fit inside a cabinet, bag, or tray. While the iodine gun is generally employed, the pad may offer a safer means. The pad is constructed using heavy cardboard or wood as a backing. One side is covered with an outward facing sticky surface, such as strips of double-back tape or self-adhesive shelf line paper affixed with the sticky backing out. Iodine crystals are spread evenly over the sticky surface and covered with a precut piece of blotting paper or thin towel. The entire pad is taped together, then is taped to the surface to be examined.

Iodine Fuming Gun

Large or immobile items can also be processed with direct iodine vapors from a source most commonly called an iodine gun. The device is a glass tube, which holds the iodine crystals through which air is passed. One method requires blowing into the tube through the rubber tubing, where heat from the breath combined with heat from the hand increases the sublimation rate of the iodine crystals. However, since moisture mixed with the iodine vapors can react with starch sizing in paper to cause a permanent blue discoloration, calcium chloride is used as a desiccant. Commercially available iodine fuming guns generally are a single tube arrangement with the iodine and calcium chloride separated by glass wool or cotton. As the calcium chloride absorbs water from the breath, it hardens and unless the tube is cleaned thoroughly after every use, the device may be rendered inoperable. An alternative design uses two tubes, as illustrated in the appendix diagram. The separate calcium chloride tube must be cleaned after use, but if neglected, a substitute tube is easily fashioned. The two-tube gun also permits easier replacement of iodine crystals during lengthy examination.

The calcium chloride tube can be omitted if a squeeze-type air bulb is used. An air bulb also prevents any possible mishap resulting from accidental inhalation when using the gun requiring breath. Air bulbs with metal valves, however, may be corroded with prolonged usage and may become inoperable. Rubber valve air bulbs do not present this problem.

Iodine fuming guns are used by heating the iodine crystals with the hand or placing the gun near a burning light bulb until purple vapor can be seen in the glass wool. The exit port of the tube is placed near the area to be examined and air is passed into the tube. Because the vapors are not contained, reactions may fade quickly, so prolonged exposure is usually required.

The following procedure is an acceptable method to develop latent impressions on human skin using iodine. This technique is employed since friction ridge skin detail is seldom discernible on human skin, and direct photography would be futile. Skin treatment with iodine vapors from a gun device will reveal a general outline only. Often a distinct shape of finger or palm contact is revealed with no apparent ridge formation. However, when a silver plate is placed over the reacted area, the absorbed iodine combines with the free silver to form silver iodide, a compound more photosensitive than silver. Transfer procedures require some practice to determine the degree of iodine exposures to the skin, but generally, allowing fading of the iodine is more effective than maximum absorption. The plate is placed with one edge adjacent to the reacted area, and a gentle, slow roll of the plate over the area is done. Complete contact without pushing or bunching the skin is required. When the pressed plate is then exposed to strong light, such as photofloods or UV lamp, the silver iodide darkens. Unnoticed detail will appear on the plate to be evaluated.

RESULTS

All iodine-developed latent impressions are transitory and must be photographically preserved as quickly as possible. Latent impressions developed through the silver transfer method will be present on the silver plate until the plate is cleaned but still should be photographically preserved.

SAFETY CONSIDERATIONS

A) Iodine is highly toxic. Vapors should be confined to a fume hood.
B) Avoid contact with skin and eyes. DO NOT BREATHE FUMES.
C) Refer to MSDS for additional information.
D) Follow proper safety precautions.

LIMITATIONS

Iodine is effective with relatively fresh oily deposits, but for those older than two weeks, the reaction may not occur or be too faint for recognition. A chemical breakdown of the oily matter appears to inhibit absorption. This time limitation of noticeable absorption and the highly successful development potential of Ninhydrin have made iodine a seldom-used procedure.

Iodine is normally not destructive and may detect deposits with insufficient amino acids for an effective Ninhydrin reaction.

Latent impressions must be photographically preserved as soon as possible.

Iodine is highly toxic and very corrosive to nearly all metals. It can be used to process nearly all types of surfaces but is normally used with porous items.

QUALITY CONTROL

The iodine crystals will be quality control tested prior to use on actual evidence. This quality control testing is to insure the desired reaction is being obtained.

LITERATURE REFERENCE

Florida Department of Law Enforcement. Latent Print Analyst Training Program, Task VII-Chemical Processing.

LCV (Leucocrystal Violet)
Category: Reagent
Reacts with: Heme groups in hemoglobin (blood)
Process product: Stains a violet color when it comes in contact with heme
Color

PURPOSE

LCV (Leucocrystal Violet) is used to enhance and develop latent prints, footwear, and tire impressions deposited in suspected blood on porous and nonporous surfaces.

MATERIALS

A) Leucocrystal Violet (dye content ≥90°)
B) 5-Sulfosalicylic Acid (Purity ≥99°)
C) Hydrogen peroxide 3%
D) Sodium Acetate
E) Scale, beakers, magnetic stirrer and stirring bar, and dark storage bottles

MIXING PROCEDURE

Formula 1

> 1000 ml 3% hydrogen peroxide
> 20 g 5-Sulfosalicylic Acid
> 7.4 g Sodium Acetate
> 2.0 g LCV

Combine above reagents in the order listed above. Store in dark bottles.

Formula 2

Solution A

> 20 g 5-Sulfosalicylic Acid
> 200 ml distilled water

Combine the above ingredients and place on a stirring device until thoroughly dissolved. Store in a dark bottle.

Solution B

> 800 ml hydrogen peroxide 3%

Combine solution A to solution B and place on a stirring device until thoroughly dissolved. Store in a dark bottle.

Solution C (Working Solution)

1.5 g Leucocrystal Violet

Add the Leucocrystal Violet (Formula 1) to the combined solutions A and B and place on a stirring device until thoroughly dissolved.

PROCESSING PROCEDURES

A) All visible prints or impressions of potential value in blood should be photographed prior to processing.
B) Utilize known blood standard, bloody print, or impression for positive control.
C) Spraying is the most effective method of application. When spraying, use the finest mist possible because excess application may cause overdevelopment or running of the blood print. Spray the target area. Development will occur within 30 s.
D) After spraying, blot the area with a tissue or paper towel. After the area is dry, the preceding steps can be repeated to possibly improve the contrast.
E) Positive control should demonstrate a change in color from reddish-brown to violet.
F) Negative control should demonstrate no color change.
G) All prints or impressions of potential value should be photographed.

SAFETY CONSIDERATIONS

A) Refer to MSDS for specified chemicals.
B) Follow proper safety precautions.
C) Use proper ventilation.
D) Wear suitable protective clothing, gloves, and goggles.
E) Avoid contact with skin and eyes.

LIMITATIONS

A) LCV is limited to the development or enhancement of suspected blood impressions.
B) When using the LCV process in direct sunlight, any developed print/impression should be photographed as soon as possible, inasmuch as photo-ionization may occur, resulting in unwanted background development.
C) Cyanoacrylate fuming may be detrimental to this process.
D) Various protein stains, such as aqueous Amido Black, etc., can be used after the LCV process.

QUALITY CONTROL

All reagent "working" solutions should be quality control tested at the time they are prepared. They should also be tested daily or prior to use on actual evidence. This quality control testing is to insure the accuracy of the mixture and that the desired reaction is being obtained.

LITERATURE REFERENCES

Federal Bureau of Investigation. Chemical Formulas and Processing Guide for Developing Latent Prints, p. 29, revised 1999.
Technical Note on Aqueous Leucocrystal Violet. Lightning Powder Company, Inc., pp. 1–4.

Lifting Materials

Category: Physical
Reacts with: No reaction
Process product: Recover powdered fingerprints

Color | **Contrasting**

PURPOSE

Lifting materials, especially tapes and opaque lifters, provide an excellent means of evidence preservation. Generally, this is secondary to photographic preservation in the laboratory. However, on occasion, the experienced examiner may elect to use lifting as the primary form of preservation for powder or particulate-developed impressions due to practical considerations concerning type of evidence, quantity of items, and time involved in photography. Such decisions must be based upon the confidence of the examiner that lifting will produce the desired result of proper and effective preservation. Any deviation from the procedure of photographic preservation followed by lifting must be based upon sound and prudent reasoning.

Properly developed and lifted impressions placed on appropriate backing material can provide excellent conditions for impression evaluation and comparison. The use of recommended backing materials will produce the required contrast, clarity, and permanence for subsequent examination procedures.

Powder and particulate-developed latent impressions should be preserved. Photographic preservation is the first and most important method and, once accomplished, may serve as the only preservation technique used in the laboratory setting. However, latent impressions developed at the crime scene and latent impressions developed on irregular-shaped items of evidence may need to be lifted to be preserved or photographed properly.

Lifting materials provide a means of capturing the developed latent impression, either to affect a transfer preservation or to protect the visualized latent on the surface once it has been photographed. Such lifting material is manufactured with an even coating of adhesive to provide specific degrees of tack or utilize substances that possess an inherent adhesive quality. Lifting material is divided into transparent and opaque devices, with each type designed for prescribed applications.

Transparent lifting material is the most widely used and is available in many variations of the same basic principle: a clear thin film with an even coating of adhesive designed to be free of defects. The simplest and most effective form is pressure wound tape produced in rolls and available in widths ranging from one to four inches. One and one-half or two-inch-wide tapes are the most popular and will provide satisfactory lifting capability for most latent impressions. The acetate film of lifting tapes can be either clear or frosted. While many experienced examiners prefer the clear, glossy tapes, such preferences may be the results of habit rather than a comparison of the properties of each. The glossy surface of clear tape may produce some glare reflection, which may present some inconvenience during examination or photographic preservation. The adhesive qualities of frosted tape are sufficient to remove the particles of a developed impression but have less of a tendency to attract loose or flaking surface material. Regardless of type, lifting tapes generally provide versatile and effective means of transfer powder or particulate-developed impressions to another surface specially selected for the purpose of preservation.

The type of preservation surface, commonly called backing material or lift cards, greatly affects the final condition and appearance of the completed lift. Generally, only two colors of backing material are required: white for dark powders and black for light powders. While any white material may be used as a lift for some occasions, specific surface properties of the backing can add clarity and contrast. Absence of noticeable fibers or other defects, uniformity in color, and high surface gloss will greatly aid in the observation of characteristics and facilitate evaluations and comparisons. Three such materials provide the best backing surface properties: commercial backings, photographic paper, and chrome coat paper.

Commercial lift cards provide the most desired characteristics of a lift backing. Available in both white and black, the backing surface is an opaque coating or resinous material that possesses high gloss, flexibility, and strength. Manufactured with superb quality control, these lift cards provide a background surface that offers the ultimate contrast to the developed powder or particulate impression.

Photographic paper designed for cold tone, general-purpose printing provides a very good lift backing surface. Resin-coated papers are especially well-suited for this purpose. Photographic paper is fixed and washed without exposure to produce high gloss white backings, or is totally exposed, fixed, and washed to yield a high gloss black backing. Medium or double-weight papers provide additional substance, which increases the durability of the backing. The only disadvantage to photographic papers is that when folded as required for side-by-side comparisons, a fracture of the emulsion may occur. While not generally harmful to the lifted latent, the fracture may result in some minute flaking and produce a highly visible line along the location of the fold. Repeated bending may even create a tear in the paper, leaving the affixed tape susceptible to potential damage.

Other materials such as unlined index cards or typing paper may be used if no other backings are available. However, routine application of these materials is discouraged.

The other category of transparent lifting material involves tow-layer devices, which provide adhesive film and the secondary preservation surface as a complete unit. Depending upon the manufacturer, such units are offered in an array of precut sheet sizes and with a choice of transparent or opaque backing surfaces.

Opaque lifting material is generally restricted to products, which are classified as rubber lifters. This type of lifter utilizes a natural low-tack quality of the synthetic rubber, which attracts the particles of a developed impression upon contact. While the tack is sufficient to successfully remove the particles in the arrangement of the residue outline, the removed particles can be disturbed on the rubber surface. Rubber lifters are supplied with an acetate cover, which is applied to the rubber surface after transfer to protect the lifted impression. Rubber lifters are available in white and black in various precut sizes. Generally, larger sections are purchased and are required to be cut into smaller sections.

MATERIALS

A) Clear fingerprint lifting tape
B) Frosted fingerprint lifting tape
C) Opaque fingerprint lifting material (rubber lifters)
D) Silicone casting material
E) Hinged fingerprint lifters
F) Black backer cards
G) White backer cards
H) Developed photo paper
I) Index cards

PROCEDURES

After photographic preservation, transparent lifting materials are generally used in routine lift preservation, while opaque lifting materials are restricted to develop impressions on curved surfaces or visible impressions created by the touching of a dusty surface. Transparent materials preserve impressions in correct position of contact, while opaque lifters produce a right-to-left inversion. Such position reversal complicates a comparison to inked impression, which most often requires a photographic intermediate procedure to return to true position. However, the high degree of flexibility inherent in the rubber material of opaque lifters permits successful transfer from irregular-shaped surfaces and round objects when acetate films will fail.

With minimum practice, lifting tapes can be easily and effectively used. A small section of the tape end is folded onto itself, adhesive to adhesive, to form a tab. The tape is then unrolled to a length slightly longer than the area to be lifted and cut from the roll. A lengthwise arc created along the tape piece may give the examiner better manipulation of the section. The cut end of the tape is pressed on the item surface at a spot adjacent to the impression, and then the fingertip is run down the center of the tape toward the tab end. If the created arc is maintained, this contact will be the only secured area to the item surface. From this center anchor, the tape is rubbed toward the edges until the entire section of tape has thorough contact.

The tape is removed by pulling the tab slowly toward the cut end. Before reaching the end, the arc should be reestablished in the tape. This will help reduce a whipping action that sometimes causes the tape to curl around and stick to itself, particularly with longer lengths. Once disengaged from the item surface, the tape is placed on an appropriate backing in the same manner, starting with the cut end.

Larger impressions may require wider tape or the use of overlapping strips. Several sections of tape may be applied with each section placed to create a slight overlap of the one next to it. When the impression is completely covered, the overlapped sections can be removed as one by grasping all tapes simultaneously. With care, the entire impression will be preserved with no missing areas.

Two-layer lifting devices are seldom used in laboratory examinations, although they have a certain degree of popularity with crime scene examiners. Designed for simplicity in operation and the convenience of a lifter and backing in one unit, they generally may yield less productive results than tapes or opaque lifters. Two general types are available: those with solid backing material and those with transparent backings. Because all are precut, a variety of sizes are available and are usually required in routine processing occasions. The end result is a collection of lifted impressions of no uniform size, some quite small and easily lost. Those in which the lifter portion is improperly repositioned to the backing present exposed adhesive, which can stick to other lifters or to containers.

Solid back lifters reveal the latent impression in true position. However, transparent backed lifters require a marking to denote the positive side. Transparent backed lifters can be photographically preserved using backlighting.

Two-layer units are used to lift impressions in the same manner as a tape except one edge is prepared to serve as a tab. The acetate film is usually less flexible than tapes and therefore, if used, is restricted to flat surfaces or those with slight regular curvature.

Opaque lifters are used by cutting out a section slightly larger than the area of the developed impression from the available sheet. The protective cover is removed and the exposed rubber section is placed gently, but firmly, onto the surface bearing the impressions. On round items, initial contact between the lifter and the surface is made at the approximate center of the impression, then the rubber material is gently shaped toward the edges. This is a difficult procedure that requires considerable practice to obtain uniform contact without lifter slippage and should only be attempted if photographic preservation is complete and secondary preservation is essential. On curved surfaces, the lifter can be rolled from one side to the other in a slow, continuous motion. Once the lift is accomplished, the plastic cover is replaced over the lifter.

SAFETY CONSIDERATIONS

Any use of latent powders produces airborne particles that represent a certain degree of health risk. Traditionally, fingerprint powders have been used with little regard for safety. Restriction of powder selection to avoid those with known toxic substances is recommended. All fingerprint processing with powders should be done in a fume hood with controllable air flow or in a well-ventilated area. In the event that no adequate hood exists or ventilation is poor, filter masks or respirators should be worn. Powder application requires appropriate safety standards, such as ventilation systems, filter masks, or respirators, and immediate cleaning of contaminated skin and clothing are essential.

Proper safety procedures will be adhered to at all times.

LITERATURE REFERENCE

Thomas, G.L., 1975. Physical methods of fingerprint development. Journal of the Canadian Forensic Science Society 8, 4.

Liquid Gun Blue
Category: Physical
Reacts with: Clean metal surface
Process product: Liquid or cold gun blue is a corrosive procedure that turns the area surrounding ridge matrix dark brown to dark blue ████████
Color ███████████

PURPOSE

Liquid Gun Blue is used to develop latent prints on brass and nickel, such as cartridge casings and coins.

MATERIALS

A) Liquid Gun Blue
B) Distilled water
C) Graduated cylinder, mixing device, beakers, and forceps

MIXING PROCEDURE

Kettner Gun Blue

0.5 ml Kettner Gun Blue
80 ml distilled water

Outers Gun Blue

0.5 ml Outers Gun Blue
20 ml distilled water

PermaBlue

0.5 ml PermaBlue
10 ml distilled water

PROCESSING PROCEDURE

The gun blue process causes a chemical reaction with the metal surface surrounding the matrix of the latent print, resulting in a reverse color print. It is recommended, but not necessary, that the items be *lightly* processed with cyanoacrylate prior to using the liquid gun blue technique.

A) Dip the item into the solution for 15–20 s.
B) Rinse the item with distilled water to stop the development process.

C) Repeat if necessary to further develop prints. Be careful to not overdevelop.

D) Allow to dry.

E) All prints of potential value should be photographed.

SAFETY CONSIDERATIONS

A) Refer to MSDS for specified chemicals.

B) Follow proper safety precautions.

C) Use proper ventilation.

D) Wear suitable protective clothing, gloves, and goggles.

E) Avoid contact with skin and eyes.

LIMITATION

Do not use on brass cartridges that are to be examined by the Firearms Section, as this process may affect their ability to conduct their examination(s).

QUALITY CONTROL

All reagent "working" solutions should be quality control tested at the time they are prepared. They should also be tested daily or prior to use on actual evidence. This quality control testing is to insure the accuracy of the mixture and that the desired reaction is being obtained.

LITERATURE REFERENCES

Saunder, G.C., June 1995. Evaluation of several techniques for developing latent fingerprints on unfired and fired cartridge cases. In: Presented at the International Symposium on Fingerprint Detection and Identification. Ne'Urim, Israel.

Russlander, H.W. "Rus", October–December 2000. Using Gun Bluing to Obtain Fingerprints on Cartridge Casings. F.D.I.A.I. Quarterly Newsletter, p. 3.

Latent Prints on Cartridge Cases, Minutiae, September–October 1995, Issue Number 32, p. 1 and 7.

Enhancement of latent prints on metal surfaces. Journal of Forensic Identification, January–February 2001, pp. 9–15.

Luminol

Category: Reagent
Reacts with: Heme groups in hemoglobin (blood)
Process product: Yellow fluorescence appears when luminol comes in contact with heme
Color [   ]

PURPOSE

Luminol is a chemical used to detect, enhance, and develop impressions in suspected blood.

MATERIALS

A) Spray bottle
B) Sodium perborate
C) 3-aminophthalhydrazide (luminol)
D) Sodium carbonate
E) Deionized or distilled water
F) Funnel

MIXING PROCEDURE

2.8 g sodium perborate
0.4 g 3-aminophthalhydrazide (luminol)
20.0 g sodium carbonate
400 ml deionized or distilled water

Mix the sodium perborate with the water. Shake well for 30–45 s. Add luminol and sodium carbonate to the mixture. Shake well for 1–2 min. Allow undissolved contents to settle to the bottom of the mixing container. Use a funnel to pour the liquid contents into the spray bottle.

PROCEDURES

A) Processing must be done in a darkened area.
B) Spray the suspected area with luminol (use fine, mist-like spray).
C) Photograph reaction.

SAFETY CONSIDERATIONS

A) Refer to MSDS for specified chemicals.
B) Follow proper safety precautions.
C) Use proper ventilation.

D) Wear suitable protective clothing, gloves, and goggles.
E) Avoid contact with skin and eyes.

LIMITATIONS

A) The use of luminol will give false positive reactions to some items, such as metals, vegetation, and some cleaning products.
B) Both negative and positive control tests should be performed prior to the use of luminol to ensure chemicals are working properly.
C) Luminol does not have a shelf life, and the working solution will be discarded after use on the day it is mixed.

QUALITY CONTROL

All reagent "working" solutions should be quality control tested at the time they are prepared. They should also be tested daily or prior to use on actual evidence. This quality control testing is to insure the accuracy of the mixture and that the desired reaction is being obtained.

LITERATURE REFERENCES

Lytle, L.T., Hedgecock, B.A. Chemiluminescence in the visualization of forensic bloodstains. Journal of Forensic Sciences, 550–562.

Zweidinger, R.A., Lytle, L.T., Pitt, C.G. Photography of bloodstains visualized by luminol. Journal of Forensic Sciences, 296–302.

MBD

Category: Dye stain
Reacts with: Bonds to cyanoacrylate residue
Process product: Fluorescent yellow stain adheres to CA residue that has polymerized to fingerprint matrix
Color [   ]

PURPOSE

MBD (7-P-methoxybenzylamino-4-nitrobenz-2 oxa-1-3-diazole) is a luminescent dye used to make cyanoacrylate-developed latent prints more visible on various colored surfaces.

MATERIALS

A) MBD
B) Methanol
C) Acetone
D) Methanol
E) 2-Propanol
F) Pentane or petroleum ether
G) Novec HFE 7100
H) Scale, beakers, graduated cylinder, magnetic stirrer and stirring bar, dark storage bottle, wash bottles, and trays
I) Forensic light source

MIXING PROCEDURE

Methanol Formula

0.03 (3/100) g MBD
1 l methanol

Thoroughly dissolve MBD in methanol using a magnetic stirrer. Store in a dark bottle.

Quick Dry Formula

0.03 (3/100) g MBD
25 ml acetone
40 ml methanol
24 ml 2-propanol
910 ml pentane or petroleum ether

Dissolve MBD in acetone. After MBD is fully dissolved, add methanol, 2-propanol, and stir. Mix MBD, acetone, methanol, and propanol solution with pentane (petroleum ether).

Nonflammable Formula

0.03 (3/100) g MBD
25 ml acetone
40 ml methanol
25 ml 2-propanol
910 ml Novec HFE 7100

Dissolve MBD in acetone. After MBD is fully dissolved, add methanol, 2-propanol, and stir. Mix MBD, acetone, methanol, and propanol solution with Novec HFE 7100.

PROCESSING PROCEDURE

A) Process the item with cyanoacrylate ester (superglue) prior to applying the MBD.
B) MBD can be applied by dipping, spraying or "washing" the solution over the surface using a chemical wash bottle.
C) Allow the item to air-dry.
D) Examine the item with a forensic light source.
E) All prints of potential value should be photographed.

SAFETY CONSIDERATIONS

A) Refer to MSDS for specified chemicals.
B) Follow proper safety precautions.
C) Use proper ventilation.
D) Wear suitable protective clothing, gloves, and goggles.
E) Avoid contact with skin and eyes.
F) When examining evidence with a forensic light source, wear protective goggles.

LIMITATION

The use of MBD is limited to nonporous surfaces that have been previously processed with cyanoacrylate.

QUALITY CONTROL

All reagent "working" solutions should be quality control tested at the time they are prepared. They should also be tested daily or prior to use on actual evidence. This quality control testing is to insure the accuracy of the mixture and that the desired reaction is being obtained.

LITERATURE REFERENCES

Cummings, H., Hollars, M., Peigare, F., Trozzi, T., November/December 1990. BBD and MBD: multipurpose reagents for latent print detection. Journal of Forensic Identification 40 (6), 334–340.

Cummings, H., Hollars, Mitchell; Trozzi, Tim, January/February 1993. Getting the most from cyanoacrylate dyes. Journal of Forensic Identification 43 (1), 37–43.

Federal Bureau of Investigation. Chemical Formulas and Processing Guide for Developing Latent Prints, pp. 54–55, revised 1999.

Fischer, John F. Forensic Light Sources and Their Use in Conjunction with Luminescent Techniques. Orange Co. Sheriff's Office.

M-Star

Category: Dye stain
Reacts with: Bonds to cyanoacrylate residue
Process product: Fluorescent orange/red stain adheres to CA residue that has polymerized to fingerprint matrix
Color ▮▮▮▮▮

PURPOSE

M-Star is a commercially prepared luminescent orange dye used to make cyanoacrylate-developed latent prints more visible using a forensic light source.

MATERIALS

A) Commercially prepared M-Star solution (in methanol)
B) Tap water
C) Trays and wash bottles
D) Forensic light source

PROCEDURES

A) Process the item with cyanoacrylate ester (superglue) prior to applying the M-Star.
B) M-Star can be applied by spraying, dipping, or "washing" the solution over the surface using a chemical wash bottle.
C) Allow 30 s to 1 min for the M-Star to penetrate the cyanoacrylate.
D) Gently rinse the item with tap water (optional).
E) Let the item dry.
F) Examine the item with a forensic light source at a range of 245–535 nm.
G) All prints of potential value should be photographed.

SAFETY CONSIDERATIONS

A) Refer to MSDS for specified chemicals.
B) Follow proper safety precautions.
C) Use proper ventilation.
D) Wear suitable protective clothing, gloves, and goggles.
E) Avoid contact with skin and eyes.
F) When examining the evidence with a light source, wear protective goggles.

LIMITATION

The use of M-Star is limited to nonporous surfaces that have been previously processed with cyanoacrylate.

QUALITY CONTROL

All reagent "working" solutions will be quality control tested at the time they are prepared. They will also be tested daily or prior to use on actual evidence.

This quality control testing is to insure the accuracy of the mixture and that the desired reaction is being obtained.

LITERATURE REFERENCES

Cummings, Harless; Hollars, Mitchell; Trozzi, Tim, January/February 1993. Getting the most from cyanoacrylate dyes. Journal of Forensic Identification 43 (1), 37–43.

Federal Bureau of Investigation. Chemical Formulas and Processing Guide for Developing Latent Prints, pp. 54–55, revised 1999.

Ninhydrin (NIN)
Category: Reagent
Reacts with: Amino acid
Process product: Ruhemann's purple color where Ninhydrin has come in contact with amino acids
Color ███████████

PURPOSE

Ninhydrin may be used to develop latent prints on porous surfaces such as paper, cardboard, and wood. Ninhydrin reacts with amino acids commonly found in latent print residue to form a purple compound, yielding visible latent prints. Ninhydrin can also be considered in the treatment of items contaminated with blood as an enhancement technique.

MATERIALS

A) Ninhydrin crystals
B) Acetone or methanol
C) Distilled water
D) Petroleum ether
E) Ethyl acetate
F) Acetic acid
G) 3M Novec Engineered Fluid HFE-7100
H) Ethanol
I) Scale, graduated cylinder, separatory funnel, pipette, dark storage bottles, wash bottles, trays, and paint brushes (nonsynthetic)
J) Mixing device
K) Chlorine bleach or ammonium hydroxide
L) Humidity cabinet and/or steam iron

MIXING PROCEDURE

0.6% Solution

25 g Ninhydrin crystals
4 l acetone or methanol
10 ml distilled water

Mix until crystals are completely dissolved. Store in a dark container.

1% Solution

10 g Ninhydrin crystals
1000 ml acetone or methanol

Mix until crystals are completely dissolved. Store in a dark container. Variations in 10 g increments of Ninhydrin crystals can be used to make a higher percentage solution.

Ninhydrin in Ether

3.75 g Ninhydrin crystals
20 ml methanol
475 ml petroleum ether

Mix until crystals are completely dissolved. Store in a dark container.

3M Novec Engineered Fluid HFE-7100 Formula

5 g Ninhydrin crystals
45 ml ethanol
2 ml ethyl acetate
5 ml acetic acid
1 l 3M Novec Engineered Fluid HFE-7100

A) Dissolve Ninhydrin crystals in ethanol.

B) Add ethyl acetate.

C) Add acetic acid.

D) Continue mixing until all the Ninhydrin has dissolved into a solution.

E) Stir in 3M Novec Engineered Fluid HFE-7100. Mix until a milky yellow solution is formed.

F) Cover and allow the solution to settle for approximately 30 min. A thin, oily-looking film may form on the top of the solution. This film consists of water, excess ethanol, and Ninhydrin and must be removed prior to use. This film can be removed by any of the following procedures:

  1) If available, process the working solution through a separatory funnel. Again, allow the solution to settle for at least 30 min. Drain the bottom phase into a squirt bottle or storage container. Stop draining when the separate, clear-looking solution nears the bottom of the funnel, or approximately 50–100 ml of solution remains in the funnel. This remaining solution should be discarded in a proper waste container for flammable solvents, as it consists of undissolved ethanol, water, and Ninhydrin.

  2) If a separatory funnel is not available, use a pipette to skim the oily film from the top, again discarding the waste in a proper waste receptacle.

  3) If neither a separatory funnel nor pipette is available, simply transfer the solution into a wash bottle. This will help insure a clean solution. When the solution level is below the straw in the wash bottle, discard the remaining solution in a proper waste receptacle.

H) Store in a dark bottle.

DESTAINING SOLUTION

One part concentrated ammonium hydroxide or chlorine bleach
Two parts distilled water or tap water

PROCESSING PROCEDURE

A) Ninhydrin solution may be applied to the item by spraying, dipping, brushing, or by the use of a chemical wash bottle inside a fume hood.
Thermal Paper
Thermal paper should be processed using the dip method and should be immersed long enough to allow all of the dark background to be washed away (usually 30s or less). Any dark background that appears after drying can be removed by rinsing with or dipping in acetone.
B) Let the item completely dry in the fume hood.
C) The postapplication environment for items processed with Ninhydrin is critical to insure an optimum chemical reaction. Heat/humidity chambers control Ninhydrin development. A near-ambient temperature to 80 degrees centigrade and a relative humidity of 70% will provide the best results.
D) Other posttreatment procedures are the use of steam irons (can cause temporary curling of paper); dry irons; and dry mount presses, which accelerate the development process.
E) A dry Ninhydrin process can be used for delicate substrates such as tissue paper. The procedure employs two pieces of clean copy paper soaked in Ninhydrin solution and then allowed to dry completely. The subject evidence is then placed between the two treated sheets and pressed together gently. Results generally take four plus hours.
F) If the stains need to be removed from the evidence, then dip the item in the destaining solution until the stains are gone. Rinse the item in distilled or tap water and let dry.
G) All prints of potential value should be photographed.

SAFETY CONSIDERATIONS

A) Refer to MSDS for specified chemicals.
B) Follow proper safety precautions.
C) Use proper ventilation.
D) Wear suitable protective clothing, gloves, and goggles.
E) Avoid contact with skin and eyes.

LIMITATIONS

A) Ninhydrin coloration is not permanent, and while some impressions have remained visible for years, others have faded in a matter of days. Photographic preservation is essential and should be accomplished as soon as possible.

B) The Ninhydrin process must be used prior to the physical developer process if both processes are being used.

QUALITY CONTROL

All reagent "working" solutions should be quality control tested at the time they are prepared. They should also be tested daily or prior to use on actual evidence. This quality control testing is to insure the accuracy of the mixture and that the desired reaction is being obtained.

LITERATURE REFERENCES

Federal Bureau of Investigation. Chemical Formulas and Processing Guide for Developing Latent Prints, pp. 30–31, revised 1999.

Home Office Scientific Research and Development Branch, 1988. Scene of Crime Handbook of Fingerprint Development Techniques, pp. 59–62.

Lee, Henry C., Gaensslen, R.E., 1991. Advances in Fingerprint Technology, pp. 104–127.

Technical Note on Ninhydrin. Lightning Powder Company, Inc., pp. 1–5.

Olsen, Robert D., 1978. Scott's Fingerprint Mechanics, pp. 276–291.

Physical Developer
Category: Reagent
Reacts with: Lipids and salts
Process product: Dark colored stain where contact is made with lipids or salts
Color ███████

PURPOSE

Physical developer (PD) is a silver-based liquid reagent that reacts with lipids, fats, oils, and waxes present in fingerprint residue.

MATERIALS

A) Physical developer—commercially prepared (solution A and solution B)
B) Maleic acid or acetic acid
C) N-Dodecylamine Acetate
D) Synperonic-N
E) Silver nitrate
F) Ferric Nitrate
G) Ferrous Ammonium Sulfate
H) Citric acid
I) Distilled water
J) Bleach
K) Four glass trays (designated for specific steps)
L) Wooden or rubber tongs
M) Mixing devices, beakers, graduated cylinders, and dark storage bottles
N) Tap water and access to a running flow of tap water
O) Oven and/or iron

MIXING PROCEDURE

Prewash (Maleic Acid)

> 25 g maleic acid
> 1000 ml distilled water

Mix the maleic acid crystals in the distilled water then store in a dark glass bottle.

Prewash (Acetic Acid)

> 150 ml acetic acid
> 850 ml distilled water

Slowly add the acetic acid to the distilled water and stir until completely mixed.

Physical Developer Solution (Commercially Prepared)

90 ml physical developer (solution B)
5 ml silver solution (solution A)

Mix thoroughly in a glass tray.

Physical Developer (Laboratory Prepared)

Stock Detergent Solution

3 g N-Dodecylamine Acetate
4 g Synperonic-N
1 l distilled water

Mix thoroughly.

Silver Nitrate Solution

20 g silver nitrate
100 ml distilled water

Mix thoroughly.

Redox Solution

60 g Ferric Nitrate
1800 ml distilled water
160 g Ferrous Ammonium Sulfate
40 g citric acid

Thoroughly mix Ferric Nitrate and water. Add Ferrous Ammonium Sulfate and mix thoroughly. Add the citric acid and mix thoroughly.

Working Solution

Add 80 ml stock detergent solution to the redox solution and mix thoroughly. Add 100 ml of the silver nitrate solution and mix thoroughly.

*Appropriate divisions can be utilized if smaller amounts of working solution are desired.

Bleach Rinse

One part bleach
One part water

PROCESSING PROCEDURE

A) Place the item to be processed in the prewash solution in a glass tray specifically designated for this step. If bubbling occurs, leave the item in the prewash until the bubbling stops.

B) Remove the item from the prewash solution and place in the physical developer solution in a glass tray specifically designated for this step. Agitate the item and periodically check for proper development. Development time can be a matter of minutes to 15 or 20 min. If the item is not developing as well as needed, a few drops of the silver solution (solution A) can be added to the physical developer.

C) Once the desired development has been reached, remove the item from the physical developer and thoroughly rinse with water.

D) Optional bleach rinse: The item can then be placed in the bleach rinse in a glass tray specifically designated for this step until the Ninhydrin stains and the background stains are removed. The item needs to be rinsed again with tap water to remove the bleach.

E) The item needs to be dried. This can be done by letting it air-dry, using a laboratory oven or iron.

F) All prints of potential value should be photographed.

SAFETY CONSIDERATIONS

A) Refer to MSDS for specified chemicals.

B) Follow proper safety precautions.

C) Use proper ventilation.

D) Wear suitable protective clothing, gloves, and goggles.

E) Avoid contact with skin and eyes.

LIMITATIONS

A) If Ninhydrin and physical developer are to be used on the same evidence, the Ninhydrin process must be done first.

B) The glassware and tongs should be specific to the process being used and not used for other processes or solutions.

C) Metal items should not be placed in the physical developer solution.

QUALITY CONTROL

All reagent "working" solutions should be quality control tested at the time they are prepared. They should also be tested daily *or* prior to use on actual evidence. This quality control testing is to insure the accuracy of the mixture and that the desired reaction is being obtained.

LITERATURE REFERENCES

Federal Bureau of Investigation. Chemical Formulas and Processing Guide for Developing Latent Prints, pp. 32–34, revised 1999.

Home Office Scientific Research and Development Branch, 1988. Scene of Crime Handbook of Fingerprint Development Techniques, pp. 63–64.

Lee, Henry C., Gaensslen, R.E., 1991. Advances in Fingerprint Technology, pp. 81–83.

Technical Note on Physical Developer. Lightning Powder Company, Inc., pp. 1–4.

Phillips, Clarence E., Cole, Douglass O., Jones, Gary W., 1990. Physical developer: a practical and productive latent print developer. Journal for Forensic Identification 40 (3), 135–147.

United States Secret Service. "Physical Developer Workshop", presented at the 82nd Annual International Association for Identification Educational and Training Conference, July 1997.

Potassium Thiocyanate

Category: Reagent
Reacts with: Iron ions
Process product: Deep red coloration when exposed to iron ions
Color ███████████

PURPOSE

Potassium Thiocyanate is a chemical used to process footwear impressions left in mud or dust. The thiocyanate ion reacts with iron ions to produce a deep red coloration.

MATERIALS

A) Potassium Thiocyanate
B) Distilled water
C) Acetone
D) Sulfuric acid

MIXING PROCEDURE

15 g Potassium Thiocyanate
15 ml distilled water
120 ml acetone
8.5 ml sulfuric acid (dilute)

The Potassium Thiocyanate is dissolved in the distilled water and acetone. The sulfuric acid is added to the solution to lower the pH because the thiocyanate test occurs most favorably in slightly acidic conditions. The addition of the acid causes potassium sulfate to be formed, which precipitates and must be removed by filtration. Remember, when mixing this chemical, always add the acid to the solution. Do not add the solution to the acid.

PROCESSING PROCEDURE

A) Apply Potassium Thiocyanate by spraying from an aerosol-powered spray in a fume cupboard (a fine mist or spray produces better detail than a heavy spray).
B) The image can be built up by repeated sprayings.
C) Running and blurring of the image can result from spraying too strongly.
D) Shelf life is probably several months, but it is advisable to make it up freshly.
E) The image should be photographed using a #58 or #61 green filter. When it is combined with high contrast black-and-white film, it will sometimes further darken and enhance the reddish-brown impression.

SAFETY CONSIDERATIONS

A) Refer to MSDS for specified chemicals.
B) Use proper ventilation.
C) Avoid contact with skin and eyes.
D) Wear suitable protective clothing, gloves, and goggles.
E) Follow proper safety precautions.

LIMITATIONS

The process should be conducted in a well-vented area.
  Running and blurring may occur if oversprayed.
  Limited shelf life.

QUALITY CONTROL

All reagent "working" solutions should be quality control tested at the time they are prepared. They should also be tested daily or prior to use on actual evidence. This quality control testing is to insure the accuracy of the mixture and that the desired reaction is being obtained.

LITERATURE REFERENCES

Bodziak, William J., 2000. Footwear Impression Evidence, second ed., pp. 145–147.
Bodziak, William J., 1990. Footwear Impression Evidence, pp. 143–144.

Powders and Particulates
Category: Physical
Reacts with: Fingerprint matrix
Process product: Powders are available in different colors and forms: standard, magnetic, and fluorescent

Color | **Various**

PURPOSE

Fingerprint powders and particulate developers are very fine particles with an affinity for moisture throughout a wide range of viscosity. Palmer perspiration, grease, oil, and most contaminants that coat the surface of friction ridge skin possess sufficient moisture and viscosity to attract and bind the fine particles together. Contact between friction ridge skin and a nonporous surface sometimes results in a transfer of the skin coating to that surface. The nonabsorbency of the surface prevents penetration by the deposited moisture.

Dependent upon the composition of the residue, the deposited moisture will range from a mostly apparent appearance to the barely perceptible or invisible appearance, even under oblique lighting. Powder or particulate application is the effort to produce or improve the appearance for preservation.

The most effective agent in terms of adherence to moisture, nonadherence to dry surfaces, particle size, uniformity, and intensity of color is carbon. Carbon is black, and as a result, black powders and particulate developers that contain carbon will consistently produce the best results. Other colored powders and particulate developers may be required due to the surface encountered. Gray powder, which usually has an aluminum base, and white powder, which usually has a chalk base, are normally used on dark-colored surfaces.

Magnetic powders are powder-coated fine iron filings subject to magnetic attraction. These adhere to moisture to a lesser degree than carbon powders but can be applied with less destructive force to the surface.

Particulate developers are substances that produce extremely fine particle residue upon burning. Materials with a high hydrocarbon content, such as camphor, pine knots, or crumbled masking tape, burn slowly and release soot in large quantities. Fine particulate carbon soot adheres extremely well to more viscous moisture, while heat from the flame softens the residue. White or light-colored soot may be produced by burning magnesium ribbon or titanium tetrachloride.

Most commercial black fingerprint powders have a high carbon base. According to the manufacturer's particular formula and production methods, the carbon base may be from a variety of sources, including lampblack, bone, or wood charcoal. Ground carbon alone cannot match the adhesion ability of fine particle soot, but commercial powders contain milled carbon of highly uniform size and shape, along with additional ingredients, to preserve the milled condition and retard air moisture absorption.

Latent print residue rests on the surface of nonporous items. The bond between the moisture and the surface depends upon the composition of the deposit, force of contact, environmental conditions during and after the transfer, and properties of the surface. Deposits largely consisting of palmer perspiration have relatively low cohesion to the surface and evaporate quickly, while those largely of sebaceous material adhere securely and remain tacky for extended periods. Surfaces such as glass, ferrous metals, or hard plastics tend to be sticky and hold residue with greater adhesion than highly polished surfaces such as chrome, stainless steel or silver. Some surfaces, such as vinyl, possess an inherent film, which inhibits secure transfer and overall moisture coating, while others, such as Formica or galvanized metal, have more texture than apparent. All conditions can affect the selection of powders and particulate developers, the method of application, and the results.

MATERIALS

A) Particulate developers (camphor, pine knots, magnesium ribbon, or titanium tetrachloride)
B) Applicators (brushes, magna-wand, or atomizer)
C) Commercially produced powders as applicable to surface
D) Forensic light source (for use with luminescent powders)

PROCEDURES

Powders may be applied by spraying with an atomizer or dropping small amounts on the surface, but the preferred procedure is the use of a brush. Fiberglass brushes are the easiest to use and maintain while permitting an application over a wider area. Powders are more effective if applied in very small amounts. While some examiners prefer pouring a supply of powder into a second container or a piece of paper, direct contact between a brush and powder container is acceptable. Only the ends of the brush bristles should be coated with the powder, and the brush should be gently tapped several times to remove all but a minimum of powder.

With the brush handle in a nearly vertical position to the surface, the bristle ends are lightly and delicately moved over the surface area. Discoloration of the print residue will usually appear immediately. With a fiberglass brush and a proper amount of powder, the impression will develop in intensity with each light pass until no further development can be observed. Even slightly excessive amounts of powder will cause a fill to occur between ridges. This fill must be removed with continued brush strokes until the impression is as free of extraneous powder as possible. However, at the first indication that the impression is being removed, all further brushing must cease.

Extraneous residue on the surface may cause a general coating effect that obscures ridge residue from the moisture coating. A lift made of the area can sometimes remove the extraneous material and permit a second application of powder. This second application may offer better contrast between the print deposit and the background.

Magnetic powder must be applied with a magnet. Wands that contain a movable magnet attract the powder when the magnet is depressed and release the powder when it is raised. Contact between powder and surface is without bristles and is more light and delicate than the fiberglass brush. Surface areas examined generally must be processed more slowly, and great care must be exercised to prevent actual contact between the end of the wand and the surface. Excessive powder can sometimes be removed by passing the magnetic wand without powder near the surface.

Particulate developers are ignited and the surface exposed to the rising soot. The surface must not be placed in the flame and must be moved to insure an even coating of particulate material. Excessive coating should be avoided. When the surface contains an adequate, even layer of soot, the surface is lightly brushed, preferably with a designated fiberglass brush, until the nonadhering soot is removed.

When processing an item of evidence with a fluorescent powder, a very small amount of powder should be placed on the fingerprint brush or magnetic wand and, in the instance of the brush, tapped against the powder container to knock the excess back into the container. The powder should be applied with a very light touch while using a forensic light source to illuminate the item. This will prevent applying too much powder to the surface, which will obliterate the ridge detail and create too much background interference.

RESULTS

Powder and particulate-developed impressions must be properly preserved. Experiments have revealed that developed impressions have a weaker adhesion to the surface than underdeveloped prints and, as a result, are more susceptible to damage from accidental contact. Photographic preservation of the developed impressions on the item affords the best preservation procedure in terms of minimal damage and complete documentation. However, lifting of the impression is just as viable a procedure as long as great care is taken during the lifting process.

SAFETY CONSIDERATIONS

A) Any use of latent powders produces airborne particles that represent a certain degree of health risk. Traditionally, fingerprint powders have been used with little regard for safety. Restriction of powder selection to avoid those with known toxic substances is recommended. All fingerprint processing with powders should be done in a fume hood with controllable air flow or in a well-ventilated area. In the event that no adequate hood exists or ventilation is poor, filter masks or respirators should be worn. Powder application requires appropriate safety standards, such as ventilation systems, filter masks, or respirators, and the immediate cleaning of contaminated skin and clothing are essential.

B) Refer to appropriate MSDS.

C) Follow proper safety precautions.

LIMITATIONS

Powder and particulate application has limited success on porous items and is normally limited to nonporous or semiporous items.

All fingerprint powders and particulate developers are indiscriminate in adhesion to moisture. Surfaces coated with residue, in addition to suspected latent prints, will attract powders and particulate developers throughout the surface.

The particle size of magnetic powder, larger than standard powder, has a tendency to paint some surfaces. Also, magnetic powders cannot effectively be used on ferrous metal surfaces.

QUALITY CONTROL

Appropriate training in the use of powders and applicators is required prior to use on actual evidence to obtain the skill necessary for proper development of latent prints.

LITERATURE REFERENCE

Florida Department of Law Enforcement, Latent Print Analyst Training Program, Task VI-Latent Print Development with Powders.

RAM

Category: Dye stain
Reacts with: Bonds to cyanoacrylate residue
Process product: Fluorescent yellow stain adheres to CA residue that has polymerized to fingerprint matrix
Color

PURPOSE

RAM is a highly luminescent dye stain used to make cyanoacrylate-developed latent prints more visible on various colored surfaces.

MATERIALS

A) Rhodamine 6G
B) Methanol
C) MBD
D) Acetone
E) Ardrox P-133D
F) Isopropyl alcohol
G) Acetonitrile
H) Petroleum ether
I) Scale, graduated cylinder, beakers, magnetic stirrer and stirring bar, and dark glass storage bottles
J) Forensic light source

MIXING PROCEDURE

Stock Solution #1

1 g Rhodamine 6G
1000 ml methanol

Combine ingredients and place on a stirring device until all the Rhodamine 6G is thoroughly dissolved.

Stock Solution #2

1 g MBD
1000 ml acetone

Combine the ingredients and place on a stirring device until all the MBD is thoroughly dissolved.

RAM WORKING SOLUTION

3 ml stock solution #1
2 ml ardrox P-133D
7 ml stock solution #2
20 ml methanol
10 ml isopropyl alcohol
8 ml acetonitrile
950 ml petroleum ether

Combine the ingredients. Do not place on a stirring device. The RAM formula must be mixed manually and in the order listed above. Store in a dark container.

PROCESSING PROCEDURE

A) Lightly fume the evidence with cyanoacrylate or in a vacuum chamber.
B) The solution can be applied by dipping, spraying, brushing, or using a chemical wash bottle.
C) Let the item dry.
D) View the item using a forensic light source, including the ultraviolet wavelengths.
E) All prints of potential value should be photographed.

SAFETY CONSIDERATIONS

A) Refer to MSDS for specified chemicals.
B) Follow proper safety precautions.
C) Use proper ventilation.
D) Wear suitable protective clothing, gloves, and goggles.
E) Avoid contact with skin and eyes.
F) When examining evidence with a light source, wear protective goggles.

LIMITATIONS

The use of RAM is limited to nonporous surfaces that have been previously processed with cyanoacrylate.

Requires the use of a forensic or UV light source.

QUALITY CONTROL

All reagent "working" solutions should be quality control tested at the time they are prepared. They should also be tested daily or prior to use on actual evidence. This quality control testing is to insure the accuracy of the mixture and that the desired reaction is being obtained.

LITERATURE REFERENCES

Cummings, H., Hollars, M., Peigare, F., Trozzi, T., RAM a Combination of Rhodamine 6G, Ardrox and MBD for Superior Enhancement of Cyanoacrylate Developed Latent Prints. Latent Fingerprint Section Research Team Federal Bureau of Investigation.

Inlow, Vici K. An Alternative Reagent for Fluorescent Dye Staining.

Rhodamine 6G Aqueous Formula

Category: Dye stain
Reacts with: Bonds to cyanoacrylate residue
Process product: Fluorescent yellow stain adheres to CA residue that has polymerized to fingerprint matrix
Color [   ]

PURPOSE

The detection of latent prints by fluorescence on nonporous surfaces previously processed with cyanoacrylate. The aqueous formula prevents the carrier in the methanol formula from bonding to clear finishes on wood surfaces such as gun stocks or grips. Bonding can cause fingerprints to be obscured due to strong background fluorescence.

MATERIALS

A) Rhodamine 6G
B) Purified water
C) Liqui-nox®
D) Glass beakers and trays
E) Magnetic stirrer
F) Scale
G) Forensic light source

FORMULA

0.05 g Rhodamine 6G
10 ml Liqui-nox®
1000 ml RO water

Combine the Rhodamine 6G and RO water in a beaker and use a magnetic stirrer until all the Rhodamine is dissolved. Add the Liqui-nox® and stir for an additional 60 s.

PROCEDURE

All items are to be cyanoacrylate fumed prior to being processed with Rhodamine 6G.

The Rhodamine is applied by dipping or through the use of a chemical wash bottle. After the items have dried, they are fluoresced by exposing them to electromagnetic energy produced by a forensic light source (using a wavelength of 515 nm) and observing them using an orange barrier filter.

RESULTS

All items were cyanoacrylate fumed prior to processing with Rhodamine 6G. Rhodamine 6G develops excellent prints that fluoresce using the forensic light source set in the 515 nm range.

SAFETY CONSIDERATIONS

A) Refer to MSDS for specified chemicals.
B) Follow proper safety precautions.
C) Use proper ventilation.
D) Wear suitable protective clothing, gloves, and goggles.
E) Avoid contact with skin and eyes.
F) When examining evidence with a light source, wear protective goggles.

QUALITY CONTROL

All reagent "working" solutions should be quality control tested at the time they are prepared. They should also be tested daily or prior to use on actual evidence. This quality control testing is to insure the accuracy of the mixture and that the desired reaction is being obtained.

LIMITATIONS

All items are to be cyanoacrylate fumed prior to being processed with Rhodamine 6G. The aqueous formula will not absorb into wood finishes or other substrates that might be affected by the methanol formula.

Requires the use of a forensic or UV light source.

LITERATURE REFERENCES

Lennard, Christopher J., Margot, Pierre A., September/October 1988. Sequencing of reagents for the improved visualization of latent fingerprints. Journal of Forensic Identification 38 (5), 197–210.

Kent, Terry (Ed.), 1993. Fingerprint Development Techniques. Heanor Gate Publisher, Derbyshire, England.

Masters, Nancy E., September/October 1990. Rhodamine 6G: taming the beast. Journal of Forensic Identification 40 (5), 265–270

Menzel, E. Roland, 1980. Fingerprint Detection with Lasers. Marcel Dekker, New York.

Menzel, E. Roland, September 1983. A Guide to Laser Latent Fingerprint Development Procedures. Identification News.

Menzel, E. Roland., 1989. Detection of latent fingerprints by laser-excited luminescence. Analytical Chemistry 61 (8), 557–561.

Tech Notes, Rhodamine 6G. Lightning Powder Company, Inc.

Rhodamine 6G Methanol Formula

Category: Dye stain
Reacts with: Bonds to cyanoacrylate residue
Process product: Fluorescent yellow stain adheres to CA residue that has polymerized to fingerprint matrix

Color [   ]

PURPOSE

The detection of latent prints by fluorescence on nonporous surfaces previously processed with cyanoacrylate.

MATERIALS

A) Rhodamine 6G
B) Methanol
C) Glass beakers and trays
D) Magnetic stirrer
E) Scale
F) Forensic light source

FORMULA

0.05 g Rhodamine 6G
1000 ml methanol

Combine the Rhodamine 6G and methanol in a beaker and use a magnetic stirrer until all the Rhodamine is dissolved.

PROCEDURE

A) All items are to be cyanoacrylate fumed prior to being processed with Rhodamine 6G.
B) The Rhodamine is applied by dipping or through the use of a chemical wash bottle. After the items have dried, they are fluoresced by exposing them to electromagnetic energy produced by a forensic light source using a wavelength of 515 nm and observing them using an orange barrier filter.

RESULTS

All items must be cyanoacrylate fumed prior to processing with Rhodamine 6G. Rhodamine 6G develops excellent prints that fluoresce brightly using the forensic light source set in the 515 nm range. Certain wood finishes and substrates may absorb the methanol-based formula, and the entire surface will fluoresce, obscuring any prints.

QUALITY CONTROL

All reagent "working" solutions will be quality control tested at the time they are prepared. They will also be tested daily or prior to use on actual evidence.

This quality control testing is to insure the accuracy of the mixture and that the desired reaction is being obtained.

LIMITATIONS

Rhodamine 6G is limited to nonporous items that have been previously processed with cyanoacrylate. Care should be taken to limit its use to items that will not be affected by the methanol carrier. Certain wood finishes and substrates may absorb the methanol-based formula, and the entire surface will fluoresce, obscuring any prints.

Requires the use of a forensic or UV light source.

SAFETY CONSIDERATIONS

A) Refer to MSDS for specified chemicals.
B) Follow proper safety precautions.
C) Use proper ventilation.
D) Wear suitable protective clothing, gloves, and goggles.
E) Avoid contact with skin and eyes.

LITERATURE REFERENCES

Lennard, Christopher J., Margot, Pierre A., September/October 1988. Sequencing of reagents for the improved visualization of latent fingerprints. Journal of Forensic Identification 38 (5), 197–210.

Kent, Terry (Ed.), 1993. Fingerprint Development Techniques. Heanor Gate Publisher, Derbyshire, England.

Masters, Nancy E., September/October 1990. Rhodamine 6G: taming the beast. Journal of Forensic Identification 40 (5), 265–270.

Menzel, E. Roland., 1980. Fingerprint Detection with Lasers. Marcel Dekker, New York.

Menzel, E. Roland., September 1983. A Guide to Laser Latent Fingerprint Development Procedures. Identification News.

Menzel, E. Roland., 1989. Detection of latent fingerprints by laser-excited luminescence. Analytical Chemistry 61 (8), 557–561.

Tech Notes, Rhodamine 6G. Lightning Powder Company, Inc.

Ruthenium Tetroxide—RTX

Category: Reagent
Reacts with: Lipids
Process product: Contact with lipids result in dark ridge detail
Color ████████

PURPOSE

The Ruthenium Tetroxide developer is capable of being applied for the development of latent prints, which are deposited on all varieties of substrates, with the exception of those substrates with black porous surfaces.

The portability of the developer makes it very convenient to use anywhere, and it is extremely easy to handle.

The RTX developer is highly sensitive to latent prints.

MATERIALS

Reagent

A) The developer is a solution of Ruthenium tetroxide (RuO_4) and HFE.
B) The developer is deep yellow, transparent, nonflammable, and does not dissolve oils. The fumes from it give off an ozonic odor and irritate the eyes and respiratory tract.

Fuming Device

A) This device is used for blowing fumes out of the developer by bubbling air up through the solution using an air pump or compressor.
B) The device is composed of a bubble glass cylinder (110 ml net), which has a cap with an air blow nozzle and a pipe for fumes to exit.

PROCEDURES

This developer method can be applied for developing prints either by a fuming method or a liquid method.

Fuming Method

There are three ways for developing latent prints using the fuming method:

Direct, Indirect, and Lifting

Direct Method

Blow the fumes out of the solution with the fumer directly on surfaces such as paper (containing thermosensitive paper), clothes, leather, wood, plastics, glass, metal, human skin, walls, and so on. The fumes react with organic compounds, particularly fatty oils or oils contained in sebaceous contaminants present in latent print residues, turning them black or brownish black. If you require more deeply developed prints, blow over again.

Indirect Method

Place the substrates in a plastic bag and then blow the fumes out in the same way as in the direct method. In the case of immovable objects such as walls, doors, etc., place plastic sheets over such objects and blow the fumes out on the top of the object. The fumes will reach the lower part of the object by being pulled down by gravity.

Soon after blowing the fumes out in the bags or under the plastic sheets, as the case may be, mix the fumes by pinching and moving back and forth with your fingertips the outside of the closed bag or the plastic sheets. The prints will appear in about two or three minutes after blowing out the fumes.

Compared with the direct method, this method requires a little more time before the prints will appear, but it does eliminate the ozonic odor and is very economical for developing prints on large substrates. The ozonic odor, which is present in plastic bags or under plastic sheets, should naturally dissipate.

Lifting Method

In the case of developing latent prints, which are deposited on human skin, metals (such as firearms), and black nonporous subjects, either soft fluorescein sheets, which are attached to wide cellophane tape strips, or sturdy fluorescein sheets are placed on the substrates where latent prints are assumed to be deposited. After strongly pressing the sheets or tapes, as the case may be, with a rubber roller only one time and then removing it, the fumes from the solution should be blown over the cellophane tape or the fluorescein sheets. Here, since developed prints appear in reverse, you should take care to identify them.

Liquid Method

Dip substrates, in particular those such as adhesive tapes, cellophane tapes, and plastic tapes with sticky surfaces, directly into the solution, which is poured into glass or ceramic vessels corresponding to the size of the particular substrate. As soon as the substrates are dipped into the solution, the images of the prints appear, particularly on the sticky surfaces.

SAFETY CONSIDERATIONS

This method of developing latent prints should be carried out before the other methods, which require the application of aluminum powder, Ninhydrin, and cyanoacrylate, etc., because these chemicals interfere with the effectiveness of the DEVELOPER or the fumes from it. After being applied to the substrates, however, the RTX does not interfere with the effectiveness of the other methods.

A) The method should be done in a fume hood with adequate ventilation or in a fume chamber.

B) Please wear plastic or rubber gloves when using the solution, or your hands will turn black. If your hands should turn black, please spray sodium hypochlorite (NaOCl) 3% aqua solution on them to remove the black stains, and wash thoroughly with water or remove the stains with alcohol.

C) The developer should absolutely not be sprayed or blown out directly toward the human face.

D) In case the sodium hypochlorite (NaOCl) solution is used on substrates, it is better that the solution and its residues are completely wiped up with either a wet cloth or paper.

E) Even though black precipitates may form on the bottom of the vessel containing the developer, as long as the solution remains pale yellow, its effectiveness will hardly vary.

F) After finishing using the developer, please put the rest of it back into another vessel, not the original vessel, and use it similarly.

G) Follow proper safety precautions.

QUALITY CONTROL

All reagent "working" solutions should be quality control tested at the time they are prepared. They should also be tested daily or prior to use on actual evidence. This quality control testing is to insure the accuracy of the mixture and that the desired reaction is being obtained.

LIMITATION

RTX does not work well on those substrates with black porous surfaces.

LITERATURE REFERENCES

Mashiko, Kenzo, Takashi Miyamoto, 1998. Latent fingerprint processing by the ruthenium tetroxide method. Journal of Forensic Identification 48,3.

Merk Index, 1982, p. 1195 (8162), says the RuO_4 fumes with the ozonic odor from the developer irritate the eyes and the respiratory tract but does not indicate that they are poisonous or toxic to humans.

MSDS, Material Safety Data Sheet, by 3M Center, St. Paul, Minnesota, says the solvent of the developer is not hazardous to the environment, poisonous, or toxic to humans, or flammable.

Safranin-O

Category: Dye stain
Reacts with: Bonds to cyanoacrylate residue
Process product: Fluorescent red/orange stain adheres to CA residue that has polymerized to fingerprint matrix
Color [＿＿＿＿＿＿＿＿]

PURPOSE

Safranin-O is a luminescent dye used to enhance cyanoacrylate-developed latent prints on nonporous surfaces.

MATERIALS

A) Safranin-O
B) Methanol
C) Scale, magnetic stirrer, and stirring bar
D) Wash bottles, trays, and sprayers
E) Forensic light source

MIXING PROCEDURE

1 g Safranin-O
1000 ml methanol

To mix Safranin-O, combine the above ingredients and place on a stirring device until all the Safranin-O is dissolved. This should take approximately 15 min.

PROCESSING PROCEDURE

A) Apply the Safranin-O to the item by dipping, spraying, or through the use of a chemical wash bottle.
B) Let the item air-dry or use a heating device.
C) Examine the item using a forensic light source.
D) All prints of potential value should be photographed.

SAFETY CONSIDERATIONS

A) Refer to MSDS for specified chemicals.
B) Follow proper safety precautions.
C) Use proper ventilation.
D) Wear suitable protective clothing, gloves, and goggles.
E) Avoid contact with skin and eyes.
F) When examining the evidence with a light source, wear protective goggles.

LIMITATION

The use of Safranin-O is limited to nonporous surfaces that have been previously processed with cyanoacrylate.

QUALITY CONTROL

All reagent "working" solutions should be quality control tested at the time they are prepared. They should also be tested daily or prior to use on actual evidence. This quality control testing is to insure the accuracy of the mixture and that the desired reaction is being obtained.

LITERATURE REFERENCE

Federal Bureau of Investigation. Chemical Formulas and Processing Guide for Developing Latent Prints, p. 61, revised 1999.

Silicone Rubber Casting
Category: Physical
Reacts with: No reaction
Process product: Castings of 3D patent prints

Color	Various

PURPOSE

Indented impressions in soft materials and extremely fragile latent impressions in media such as dust limited the preservation procedure to photography for many years. The development of silicone-based casting materials has provided a viable method to preserve indented impressions. Characteristics of these materials permit replication of even the most minute depressions without the generation of heat and with minimal shrinkage. The silicone base is a thick liquid that requires the introduction of a catalyst to harden and, once set, forms a very strong, rubbery substance, which releases easily from the mold. The catalyst reacts with the silicone base slowly, usually in three to seven minutes. During this time, the liquid will flow with minimal disturbance to cover the surface. As a result, silicone rubber casting materials have been used to successfully lift powder or particulate-developed impressions from concave surfaces and, with the use of an enclosing dam, dust impressions from any surface. The remarkable replication ability of these materials also has been utilized in recording friction ridge skin of deceased individuals when the conventional methods were difficult or unwarranted.

Silicone rubber casting materials are available from many manufacturers and are used often by toolmark examiners. However, materials available in paste form, which tend to require a spatula for application, are not appropriate for latent print impression casting. Duplicast™, a brand first marketed for latent print use, is reported generally quite reliable and consistent for all preservation procedures.

MATERIALS

Commercial silicone rubber casting material, which may include, but is not limited to, Duplicast™, Mikrosil™, or Accutrans™ (polyvinylsiloxane).

PROCEDURES

Any use of silicone rubber casting material must be preceded by all available photographic means to adequately preserve the impression. Indented impressions developed or visible in a concave surface often can be cast using the substance as a mold. Impressions on flat or concave surfaces and very shallow indented impressions may require the construction of a retaining dam. Any pliable substance, such as clay, is acceptable.

A sufficient quantity of the silicone rubber base for filling the indentation, or producing a cast of about one-eighth inch thick, is poured into a container. Additional depth of the cast offers no benefit. Smaller amounts of catalyst increase the setting time, which may be advantageous for casting larger areas or with fragile surfaces. After the catalyst is added, the substance is thoroughly mixed using a tongue depressor or similar instrument, and the solution is gently poured onto the area. The mixing instrument may be used to push the liquid out of the container but must not be used to force the fluid into any area of the mold. When firm, the cast is removed.

In order to record *friction ridge skin*, the mixture is prepared using the least required amount of catalyst and applied directly to the skin using the mixing instrument to gently spread the material to form an even coating. By obtaining a thin, uniform application, the material will not run and may be spread on vertical or upside down areas with relative ease. Once set, the rubber may be gently peeled from the skin surface.

RESULTS

Casts of indented impressions, fragile substances, and powder or particulate-developed impressions are similar to opaque lifting material preservations in that position is reversed. Casts of friction ridge skin reveal depressed ridges and raised furrows, as well as reversed positioning. Most casts can be easily photographed. A light coating of fingerprint ink may aid to increase the contrast of indented impressions. Casts of friction ridge skin may be photographed successfully using low angle oblique lighting. The durability of the casting material permits excellent preservation in support of initial photography.

SAFETY CONSIDERATIONS

A) Refer to appropriate MSDS.
B) Follow proper safety precautions.

LIMITATION

Nearly any type of substrate can be successfully cast except those cooled to a temperature below 40 °F. Casts made in a substance similar to the silicone base, such sealers or silicone-based caulks, require the application of a releasing agent to the surface prior to casting. Commercial products are available; however, a light coating with a glass cleaner spray, such as Windex™, will work well.

QUALITY CONTROL

All silicone rubber products have a shelf life, and an expiration date should be listed. Use after the expiration date is not recommended.

Training should be conducted in the use of silicone rubber casting prior to application on items of evidence.

Instructions provided by the manufacturer should be followed to ensure proper results.

LITERATURE REFERENCE

Technical Notes, Impression Evidence. Lightning Powder Company, Inc., 1998, p. 2–3.

Silver Nitrate
Category: Reagent
Reacts with: Sodium
Process product: Dark brown stain where contact was made with sodium
Color ███████████

PURPOSE

Silver nitrate is used to develop latent prints on porous items. It reacts with the sodium chloride or salt content in perspiration.

MATERIALS

A) Silver nitrate
B) Distilled water
C) Ethyl alcohol
D) Mercuric nitrate
E) Nitric acid
F) Scale, graduated cylinder, beakers, dark storage bottle, magnetic stirrer, and stirring bar
G) Sprayers, trays, paint brushes (nonsynthetic), and swabs
H) Lamps

MIXING PROCEDURE

3% Water Base Solution

30 g silver nitrate crystals
1000 ml distilled water

Combine the silver nitrate and distilled water and place on a stirring device for approximately 10 min or until all the crystals are dissolved.

10% Water Base Solution

100 g silver nitrate crystals
1000 ml distilled water

Combine the silver nitrate and distilled water and place on a stirring device for approximately 10 min or until all the crystals are dissolved.

*The concentration percentage on the water base solution can be increased or decreased by varying the amount of silver nitrate crystals accordingly.

3% Alcohol Base Solution

30 g silver nitrate crystals
100 ml distilled water
1000 ml ethyl alcohol

Combine the silver nitrate and distilled water and place on a stirring device until all the crystals are dissolved. Add this solution to the ethyl alcohol.

Mercuric Nitrate 20% Destaining Stock Solution

400 g mercuric nitrate crystals
0.45 cc nitric acid
1 quart distilled water

Mercuric Nitrate 2% Destaining Working Solution

380 cc 20% mercuric nitrate stock solution
1 gallon distilled water

PROCESSING PROCEDURE

A) When applying the silver nitrate solution to an item, it can be dipped, sprayed, painted, or swabbed with the solution until thoroughly saturated.
B) Blot the item, removing all excess liquid.
C) Let the item completely dry.
D) Expose the item to a high-intensity light, such as a photoflood or UV lamp. Sunlight can also be used, but darkening may be too rapid to control.
E) Chemical development can be accomplished by using photographic developer designed for papers. The treated item is washed, then placed in the normal developer solution. When optimum intensity is reached, the item is removed, washed, and dried.
F) Latent prints should be photographed as quickly as possible, as continued exposure to light will eventually darken the surface of the item.
G) The item can then be destained by dipping in the mercuric nitrate 2% destaining solution and then rinsing with distilled water.
H) All prints of potential value should be photographed.

SAFETY CONSIDERATIONS

A) Refer to MSDS for specified chemicals.
B) Follow proper safety precautions.
C) Use proper ventilation.
D) Wear suitable protective clothing, gloves, and goggles.
E) Avoid contact with skin and eyes.

LIMITATIONS

A) If Ninhydrin and silver nitrate are both to be used on the item, the Ninhydrin must be used prior to the silver nitrate.

B) Silver nitrate is limited for use on porous surfaces.

QUALITY CONTROL

All reagent "working" solutions should be quality control tested at the time they are prepared. They should also be tested daily or prior to use on actual evidence. This quality control testing is to insure the accuracy of the mixture and that the desired reaction is being obtained.

LITERATURE REFERENCES

Cowger, James F., 1983. Friction Ridge Skin, pp. 99–102.

Federal Bureau of Investigation. Chemical Formulas and Processing Guide for Developing Latent Prints, pp. 35–36, revised 1999.

Home Office Scientific Reasearch and Development Branch, 1988. Fingerprint Development Techniques, pp. 73–74.

Lee, Henry C., Gaensslen, R.E., 1991. Advances in Fingerprint Technology, p. 79.

Moenssens, Andre A., 1971. Fingerprint Techniques, pp. 120–121.

Olsen, Robert D., 1978. Scott's Fingerprint Mechanics, pp. 291–308.

Small Particle Reagent

Category: Physical
Reacts with: Fingerprint matrix
Process product: Various colors and types of powder are suspended in liquid and sprayed onto evidence, and powder particles adhere to matrix

Color	Various

PURPOSE

Small Particle Reagent (SPR) was developed and refined by the British Home Office as an effective procedure for processing wet surfaces. Both porous and nonporous surfaces, which are wet at the time of latent print deposit or become wet after deposit, seldom retain sufficient water-soluble material for conventional processing methods. Nonporous items that have been allowed to dry offer some potential if the deposit contains nonwater-soluble oily mater, but the drying process lessens the possibility of adequate adhesion for powder or particulates. Porous items present even less likelihood. Molybdenum disulfide is a lipid-sensitive reagent, and lipid material is not water soluble. This particular method is used to develop latent impressions that are wet or contain residues that would make processing with a brush difficult.

Recent refinements in the surfactant solution have not only improved the uniformity of suspension but have increased the application of SPR to other surfaces. SPR is very effective in the secondary treatment of cyanoacrylate ester-developed impressions by adhering to faint impressions generally better than powders and particulates and provides the best approach to processing water-soaked papers.

The luminescent SPR reagent works best without treatment with cyanoacrylate.

MATERIALS

Premixed SPR reagent is available commercially in black, white, and luminescent solutions or can be mixed in the laboratory using the following materials:

A) Scales
B) Graduated cylinders
C) Beakers
D) Magnetic stirrer and stirring rod
E) Trays
F) Wash bottle

G) Spray bottle
H) Half-gallon bottle
I) Water
J) Photo-Flo™200
K) Molybdenum Disulfide
L) Forensic light source (for use with the luminescent SPR)

MIXING PROCEDURE

Measure 1 l of water into the half-gallon bottle. Distilled water is preferred, but ordinary tap water should work well in most areas.

Add 30 g of Molybdenum Disulfide to the liter of water. Add two or three drops of Kodak Photo-Flo™200 to enable the Molybdenum Disulfide powder to mix into the solution. Do not add extra Photo-Flo.

Place lid on bottle and shake mixture until there is no powder floating on the surface (approximately 3–5 min).

SPR is also commercially available in packets that require only that they be mixed in water. Follow the manufacturer's mixing instructions.

PROCESSING PROCEDURES

Regardless of whether or not the SPR solution is premixed or mixed in the laboratory, the processing procedures are the same.

A) The solution may be sprayed onto the surface or the item may be dipped into a tray containing the SPR solution.
B) The solution is poured into a shallow dish, such as a photography tray, to a depth sufficient to cover the item for processing and should be stirred immediately before the item is introduced. For nonporous articles, the item is simply placed in the liquid to lie as flat as possible and allowed to remain for approximately 30 s. When removed, the item is placed in a second tray filled with clear tap water. It may be gently agitated, or a flow may be established. The excess SPR will wash off readily. The procedure should be repeated to process the remaining surfaces and allowed to dry.
C) Water-soaked paper is processed in a like manner, except the tray should be gently rocked during the entire immersion time.
D) Items may be processed by using a spray wash bottle. The solution is simply sprayed over the surface in a flow and followed by a second wash of clear tap water. For outdoor application of very large items, such as a wet automobile, a garden sprayer can be used. Generally light to moderate flows of rinse water will not dislodge the SPR particles.

RESULTS

The developed impressions should be photographically preserved. Once satisfactory photographs have been obtained, let the surface dry and lift the prints if desired. If necessary, the impressions can be lifted while the surface is still wet; however, it is easier if the surface can be allowed to dry.

Undiluted SPR solution may be captured and reused with no degradation of effectiveness, but a badly contaminated solution should be discarded.

SAFETY CONSIDERATIONS

A) SPR presents no real health hazard, although skin irritation may occur with prolonged contact.
B) Refer to appropriate MSDS.
C) Follow proper safety precautions.

LIMITATION

Molybdenum disulfide is produced in various particle sizes, which are generally not listed. Smaller particle size is more effective.

QUALITY CONTROL

Small Particle Reagent will be quality control tested prior to use on actual evidence. This quality control testing is to insure the desired reaction is being obtained.

LITERATURE REFERENCES

Police Scientific Development Branch, Home Office Policing and Crime Reduction Group, 2000. Fingerprint Development Handbook.

Florida Department of Law Enforcement, Latent Print Analyst Training Program, Task VII-Chemical Processing.

Technical Notes, Chemical Processing For Latent Prints. Lighting Powder Company, 1998.

Sticky-Side Powder

Category: Physical

Reacts with: Fingerprint matrix

Process product: Various colors and types of powder are mixed with liquid and painted on adhesive surfaces, and powder particles adhere to matrix

Color | **Various**

PURPOSE

Sticky-side Powder is used to process the sticky side of adhesive tapes and labels for latent prints. Sticky-side Powder™ is available in a commercial form or can be mixed in the laboratory using regular fingerprint powders. Ash gray and Redwop are particularly useful on dark-colored and black tape.

MATERIALS

A) Commercially available Sticky-side Powder™, Ash gray powder, or Lightning® black powder

B) Photo-Flo™ 200 or Photo-Flo™ 600 solution

C) Liqui-Nox™ concentrated liquid detergent

D) Petri or shallow dish

E) Distilled water

F) Camel-hair or small brush

G) Tap water

MIXING PROCEDURE

Commercial Sticky-Side Powder™

1 tsp. Sticky-side Powder™

Photo-Flo™ solution

Place the Sticky-side Powder™ in a petri or shallow dish. A small amount of Photo-Flo™ 200 must be diluted with distilled water by 50% to make Photo-Flo™ 100. Add Photo-Flo™ 100 solution to the powder and stir until mixture is the consistency of thin paint.

Alternate Black Powder

1 tsp. Lightning® black powder

40 drops Liqui-Nox™ solution (diluted 50:50 with water)

Combine the Lightning® black powder and Liqui-Nox™ solution in a shallow dish and stir until the solution has the consistency of shaving cream. Note: *Redwop®* can be substituted for black powder for use on dark-colored tapes.

Ash Gray Powder

1 tsp Ash gray powder
Photo-Flo™ 200 or Photo-Flo™ 600 solution

Place the ash gray powder in a petri or shallow dish. Add a small amount of Photo-Flo™ solution to the powder and stir until the mixture is the consistency of thin paint.

PROCESSING PROCEDURE

The solutions are painted on the adhesive surface of the tape with a camel-hair or small brush. Allow to set for approximately 30–60 s, then rinse off the solution with a slow stream of cold tap water. Allow to dry. Repeat procedure if necessary.

SAFETY CONSIDERATIONS

A) A dust mask is recommended when measuring the powder to prevent inhalation of particles.
B) Once mixed, the material should not be ingested.
C) Refer to appropriate MSDS.
D) Follow proper safety precautions.

LIMITATION

This procedure is limited to the adhesive side of tapes and labels. Alternate appropriate methods should be applied to the nonadhesive side. Mix for each application or daily.

QUALITY CONTROL

Sticky-side Powder will be quality control tested prior to use on actual evidence. This quality control testing is to insure the desired reaction is being obtained.

LITERATURE REFERENCES

U. S. Department of Justice, Federal Bureau of Investigation, Laboratory Division, 2000. Processing Guide for Developing Latent Prints.
Technical Notes, Chemical Processing for Latent Prints. Lighting Powder Company, 1998.
Validation Test for the sticky-side powder process, conducted by the Latent Print Section, Tampa Bay Regional Operations Center, Florida Department of Law Enforcement, 051, 500–051, 800.

Sudan Black

Category: Physical
Reacts with: Fingerprint matrix
Process product: Sudan black is suspended in liquid, and evidence is dipped into the solution; powder particles adhere to matrix
Color ████████

PURPOSE

Sudan Black is a dye that stains the fatty components of sebaceous secretions. It is one of the best processes for developing latent prints on smooth or rough nonporous surfaces contaminated with greasy or sticky substances. It can be used on waxy surfaces, such as candles or wax-paper milk cartons.

MATERIALS

A) Sudan Black
B) Ethyl alcohol
C) Distilled water
D) Scale, graduated cylinder, beaker, glass bottles, and trays
E) Access to running tap water

MIXING PROCEDURE

15 g Sudan Black
1000 ml ethyl alcohol
500 ml distilled water

Weigh out Sudan Black and place in a clean beaker. Add ethanol and stir. Then add the distilled water and stir until thoroughly mixed. Some of the Sudan Black will not dissolve. Some will remain as particulate matter floating in the solution or will appear as sediment. Pour the solution, including any solid matter, into a clean glass bottle with a tight-fitting cap.

PROCESSING PROCEDURE

A) Shake the Sudan Black solution and pour a sufficient amount into a tray large enough to place the item of evidence. (If the item is too large for a tray, the solution can be poured over the surface repeatedly for about two to three minutes.)
B) Soak the item for two to three minutes.
C) Rinse the article in cool, running tap water.
D) Allow the item to dry at room temperature.
E) Evaluate the latent prints only after they have completely dried.

F) Faintly developed latent prints can sometimes be enhanced by reprocessing.

G) All prints of potential value should be photographed.

SAFETY CONSIDERATIONS

A) Refer to MSDS for specified chemicals.

B) Follow proper safety precautions.

C) Use proper ventilation.

D) Wear suitable protective clothing, gloves, and goggles.

E) Avoid contact with skin and eyes.

LIMITATION

This item is limited to the development of latent prints on nonporous items. Do not use this process on porous or absorbent items, as the entire item will be stained a dark color. This process may run inks and interfere with blood and body fluid examinations.

QUALITY CONTROL

All reagent "working" solutions should be quality control tested at the time they are prepared. They should also be tested daily or prior to use on actual evidence. This quality control testing is to insure the accuracy of the mixture and that the desired reaction is being obtained.

LITERATURE REFERENCES

Federal Bureau of Investigation. Chemical Formulas and Processing Guide for Developing Latent Prints, p. 41, revised 1999.

Home Office Scientific Research and Development Branch, 1988. Fingerprint Development Techniques, pp. 79–80.

Technical Note on Sudan Black. Lightning Powder Company, Inc., pp. 1–3.

Tape-Glo™

Category: Dye stain
Reacts with: Fingerprint matrix
Process product: Fluorescent yellow/green ridges on adhesive surfaces
Color ☐

PURPOSE

Tape-Glo™ is a fluorescent dye for developing latent prints on the adhesive side of tape. After treatment, a forensic light source (i.e., CrimeScope) is used to visualize the latent prints. Tape-Glo™ is a premixed solution and is safe to use in the laboratory without the use of a fume hood.

MATERIALS

A) Commercially available premixed Tape-Glo™
B) Plastic or glass tray
C) Distilled water

PROCEDURES

Processing Procedures for Plastic-Backed Adhesive Tapes

Place the tape in the tray with the adhesive side up. Pour enough Tape-Glo™ over the tape for sufficient coverage. Tape-Glo™ should remain on the tape approximately 10–15 s. Remove tape and rinse with distilled water. It is not necessary to allow the tape to dry before viewing under a forensic light source.

Processing Procedures for Cloth or Paper-Backed Adhesive Tapes

Place the tape in a container of fresh distilled water. Allow the tape to become saturated, about 30 s. Then follow the instructions for plastic-backed adhesive tapes.

Dim room lights and examine tape for latent prints by using either the 495 or 515 nm settings on the CrimeScope or other forensic light source with comparable wavelength settings. View tape and photograph using orange goggles or filters.

SAFETY CONSIDERATIONS

A) Refer to appropriate Material Safety Data Sheet (MSDS) for Tape-Glo™, Lightning Powder Company, Inc.
B) Follow proper safety precautions.

QUALITY CONTROL

Tape-Glo™ will be quality control tested prior to use on actual evidence. This quality control testing is to insure the desired reaction is being obtained.

LITERATURE REFERENCES

Technical Note, Tape Glo™ Fluorescent Dye. Lighting Powder Company. http://redwop.com/technotes.asp?ID=109.

Technical Notes, Tape Glo™ Fluorescent Dye. Lightning Powder Company, April 2000.

LumaChem, Inc., *Tape Glo™ Latent Print Developer for Sticky Side Tape,* September 1999.

> **Thermal Paper Destaining Solution**
> Category: Chemical
> Reacts with: Print ink
> Process product: Clears stains that result from amino acid processes
> Color | **None**

PURPOSE

The purpose of this process is to clear dark background staining from thermal paper. Processing thermal paper by spraying with Ninhydrin (NIN) acetone based, NIN HFE based, or a Ninhydrin analog, such as DFO or IND, will in most cases result in the background turning dark, if not black, thus obscuring the NIN prints.

MATERIALS

A) Acetone
B) Methanol
C) Wash bottle
D) Tray
E) Exhaust hood

FORMULA

Acetone or methanol

PROCEDURE

In an exhaust hood, wash acetone or methanol over thermal paper that has been previously processed with Ninhydrin or a Ninhydrin analog, such as DFO or IND, until the dark background stains have been washed away. The thermal paper can also be dipped in a tray of acetone or methanol. Let dry.

RESULTS

The acetone or methanol washes away the dark staining that occurs when thermal paper is processed with NIN or Ninhydrin analogs such as IND. This allows the developed print to be observed just as it would have been on standard white paper. The carrier/solvent wash *does not* interfere with the fluorescent properties of IND.

LIMITATION

Extended exposure to the carrier/solvent will have a tendency to slightly fade the NIN print, so only wash or dip the evidence long enough to remove the background (5–10 s). The process can be repeated if the dark background has not completely cleared after drying.

SAFETY CONSIDERATIONS

A) Refer to MSDS for specified chemicals.
B) Follow proper safety precautions.
C) Use proper ventilation.
D) Wear suitable protective clothing, gloves, and goggles.
E) Avoid contact with skin and eyes.

LITERATURE REFERENCES

Home Office, Police Scientific Development Branch, Manual of Fingerprint Development Techniques, second ed., revised January 2001, second revision August 2004, Chapter 4, Ninhydrin & DFO, p. 6, sect 7.3.
Internet site: http://clpex.com/phpBB/viewtopic.php?t=213.

TMB (Tetramethylbenzidine)
Category:
Reacts with:
Process product:
Color ▮▮▮▮▮▮

PURPOSE

TMB is used to develop latent prints, footwear, and tire impressions that may be in blood.

MATERIALS

A) Sodium Acetate
B) Glacial acetic acid
C) Distilled water
D) 3,3′,5,5′-tetramethylbenzidine (TMB)
E) Collodion
F) Ethanol
G) Ethyl ether
H) Sodium perborate
I) Scale, graduated cylinder, beakers, magnetic stirrer and stirring bar, and spray bottle

MIXING PROCEDURES

Acetate Buffer Solution

10 g Sodium Acetate
86 ml glacial acetic acid
100 ml distilled water

Dissolve Sodium Acetate in glacial acetic acid. Add distilled water.

TMB Stock Solution

1 g TMB
50 ml acetate buffer solution

Dissolve TMB in acetate buffer. Thoroughly mix for 5 min, then filter the solution to remove any undissolved particles.

Collodion-Ethanol-Ether Solution

150 ml collodion
75 ml ethanol
600 ml ethyl ether

Mix collodion in ethanol. Let stand for five minutes. While stirring constantly, slowly add ethyl ether.

TMB Working Solution

1 g sodium perborate
12 ml TMB stock solution
240 ml collodion-ethanol-ether solution

Mix sodium perborate in TMB stock solution. Add collodion-ethanol-ether solution. Mix well.

PROCESSING PROCEDURE

A) All visible prints or impressions of potential value in blood should be photographed prior to processing.
B) Blood should be completely dry or fixed prior to processing.
C) Lightly spray TMB two or three times at a distance of 10–12 inches from the specimen.
D) Blood residue will turn a greenish-blue color.
E) The area can be sprayed again to continue the development, but proceed cautiously. If an area is sprayed too heavily, it may turn the whole area a dark blue, and any ridge detail may be lost.
F) All prints or impressions of potential value should be photographed.

SAFETY CONSIDERATIONS

A) Refer to MSDS for specified chemicals.
B) Follow proper safety precautions.
C) Use proper ventilation.
D) Wear suitable protective clothing, gloves, and goggles.
E) Avoid contact with skin and eyes.
F) Benzine is a known carcinogen.

LIMITATION

TMB is limited to the use of items contaminated with suspected blood.

QUALITY CONTROL

All reagent "working" solutions should be quality control tested at the time they are prepared. They should also be tested daily or prior to use on actual evidence. This quality control testing is to insure the accuracy of the mixture and that the desired reaction is being obtained.

LITERATURE REFERENCES

Hamm, Ernest D., June 1983. Enhancement and Development of Blood Prints. In: Paper presented at the Georgia State Division of the International Association for Identification Workshop.

Lee, Henry C., Gaensslen, R.E., 1991. Advances in Fingerprint Technology, pp. 84–85.

Lee, Henry C., March 1984. TMB as an Enhancement Reagent for Bloody Prints. Identification News, pp. 10–11.

Nutt, Jim, February 1985. Chemically Enhanced Bloody Fingerprints. FBI Law Enforcement Bulletin, pp. 22–25.

Wetwop™

Category: Physical
Reacts with: Fingerprint matrix on adhesive
Process product: Adhesive process
Color [   ] ███████

PURPOSE

Wetwop™ is used for developing latent prints on the sticky side of tapes and labels. The solution will stain latent print residue deposited on adhesive surfaces. The developed prints are visible under ambient light. Wetwop™ is a premixed solution and is safe to use in the laboratory without the use of a fume hood.

MATERIALS

A) Commercially available, premixed Wetwop™
B) Paint brush
C) Tap water

PROCEDURES

Shake the Wetwop™ bottle thoroughly. Apply Wetwop™ to the adhesive side of tape using a paintbrush. Wetwop™ should remain on the tape approximately 10–20 s. Rinse the tape with a gentle stream of cool tap water until the water runs clear. Allow the tape to dry.

Latent prints are visually examined under ambient light.

SAFETY CONSIDERATIONS

A) Refer to appropriate Material Safety Data Sheet (MSDS) for Wetwop™, Lightning Powder Company.
B) Follow proper safety precautions.

LIMITATION

This procedure is limited to the adhesive side of tapes and labels. Alternate appropriate methods should be applied to the nonadhesive side.

QUALITY CONTROL

Wetwop™ will be quality control tested prior to use on actual evidence. This quality control testing is to insure the desired reaction is being obtained.

LITERATURE REFERENCES

Technical Note, Wetwop™ - Black/White. Lighting Powder Company. http://
redwop.com/technotes.asp?ID=124.
Product Site, Wetwop™. Lightning Powder Company. http://shop.optemize.
com/shop/merchant.mv?Screen=PROD&Store_Code=RedWop&Product_
Code=1-0077.

Zinc Chloride
Category: Stain
Reacts with: Ninhydrin
Process product: Fluorescent prints
Color [   ]

PURPOSE

Zinc Chloride is a chemical process used after the Ninhydrin process to enhance weak Ninhydrin prints with the use of a forensic light source.

MATERIALS

A) Zinc chloride
B) Methanol
C) Scale, graduated cylinder, mixing device, and sprayer
D) Forensic light source

MIXING PROCEDURE

2 g zinc chloride
100 ml methanol

Dissolve zinc chloride in methanol using a magnetic stirrer.

PROCESSING PROCEDURE

A) Application to the Ninhydrin-treated surface must be by extremely light spraying of the zinc chloride solution. Care must be exercised to avoid a visible wetting of the surface since nearly all solvents can diffuse the Ninhydrin impression.
B) After initial exposure of the lightest possible mist, several seconds are allowed for a reaction, which is indicated by a color change from purple to orange-red.
C) Successive light applications may be required, but once the color shift occurs, no further exposure to the zinc chloride is necessary.
D) Examine the specimen using a forensic light source in the 450–515 nm range and an orange blocking filter.
E) Latent prints of potential value should be photographed as quickly as possible since they may fade rapidly.

SAFETY CONSIDERATIONS

A) Refer to MSDS for specified chemicals.
B) Follow proper safety precautions.

C) Use proper ventilation.

D) Wear suitable protective clothing, gloves, and goggles.

E) Avoid contact with skin and eyes.

F) When examining evidence with a light source, use the proper goggles.

LIMITATION

The use of zinc chloride is limited to the processing of porous items that have been previously processed with Ninhydrin.

QUALITY CONTROL

All reagent "working" solutions should be quality control tested at the time they are prepared. They should also be tested daily or prior to use on actual evidence. This quality control testing is to insure the accuracy of the mixture and that the desired reaction is being obtained.

LITERATURE REFERENCES

Herod, D.W., Menzel, E.R., July 1982. Laser detection of latent fingerprints: ninhydrin followed by zinc chloride. Journal of Forensic Sciences, 513–518.

Kobus, H.J., Stoilovic, M., Warrener, R.N., 1983. A simple luminescent post-ninhydrin treatment for the improved visualization of fingerprints on documents in cases where ninhydrin alone gives poor results. Forensic Science International 22, 161–170.

Appendix A

TABLE 1: WEIGHTS, MEASURES, AND TEMPERATURE

kiloliter…kL	1 kL = 1000 L
liter…L	1 L = 1000 mL
milliliter…mL	1 mL = 0.001 L
kilogram…kg	1 kg = 1000 g
gram…g	1 g = 1000 mg
milligram…mg	1 mg = 0.001 g
gallon…gal	1 gal = 4 qt = 3.785 L
quart…qt	1 qt = 2 pt = 0.946 L
pint…pt	1 pt = 473.176 mL
atmosphere…atm	1 atm = 760 torr @ 14.7 pounds per square inch (psi)
teaspoon…tsp	1 tsp = 4.92892 mL

Converting from Fahrenheit (°F) to Celsius (°C)
$$tC = 5/9 \ (tF - 32)$$
Converting from Celsius (°C) to Fahrenheit (°F)
$$tF = 9/5 \ (tC + 32)$$

TABLE 2: CONVERSION MULTIPLIERS

From Standard/US Customary Units
To SI/Metric Units

Symbol	When You Know	Multiply by	To Find	Symbol
Length				
in	inches	25.4	millimeters	mm
ft	feet	0.305	meters	m
yd	yards	0.914	meters	m
mi	miles	1.61	kilometers	km
Area				
in^2	square inches	645.2	square millimeters	mm^2
ft^2	square feet	0.093	square meters	m^2
yd^2	square yard	0.836	square meters	m^2
ac	acres	0.405	hectares	ha
mi^2	square miles	2.59	square kilometers	km^2

Continued

From Standard/US Customary Units
To SI/Metric Units

Symbol	When You Know	Multiply by	To Find	Symbol
Volume				
fl oz	fluid ounces	29.57	milliliters	mL
gal	gallons	3.785	liters	L
ft^3	cubic feet	0.028	cubic meters	m^3
yd^3	cubic yards	0.765	cubic meters	m^3
Mass				
oz	ounces	28.35	grams	g
lb	pounds	0.454	kilograms	kg
T	short tons (2000 lb)	0.907	megagrams (or "metric ton")	Mg (or "t")
Temperature				
°F	Fahrenheit	(F-32) × 5/9 or (F-32)/1.8	Celsius	°C
Illumination				
fc	foot-candles	10.76	lux	lx
fl	foot-lamberts	3.426	candela/m^2	cd/m^2
Force and Pressure or Stress				
lbf	poundforce	4.45	newtons	N
lbf/in^2	poundforce per square inch	6.89	kilopascals	kPa

From SI/Metric Units
To Standard/US Customary Units

Symbol	When You Know	Multiply by	To Find	Symbol
Length				
mm	millimeters	0.039	inches	in
m	meters	3.28	feet	ft
m	meters	1.09	yards	yd
km	kilometers	0.621	miles	mi
Area				
mm^2	millimeters	0.0016	square inches	in^2
m^2	square meters	10.764	square feet	ft^2
m^2	square meters	1.195	square yards	yd^2
ha	hectares	2.47	acres	ac
km^2	square kilometers	0.386	square miles	mi^2
Volume				
mL	milliliters	0.034	fluid ounces	fl oz
L	liters	0.264	gallons	gal
m^3	cubic meters	35.314	cubic feet	ft^3
m^3	cubic meters	1.307	cubic yards	yd^3
Mass				
g	grams	0.035	ounces	oz
kg	kilograms	2.202	pounds	lb
Mg (or "t")	megagrams (or "metric ton")	1.103	short tons (2000 lb)	T

From SI/Metric Units
To Standard/US Customary Units

Symbol	When You Know	Multiply by	To Find	Symbol
Temperature				
°C	Celsius	$1.8\,°C + 32$	Fahrenheit	°F
Illumination				
lx	lux	0.0929	foot-candles	fc
cd/m^2	candela/m^2	0.2919	foot-lamberts	fl
Force and Pressure or Stress				
N	newtons	0.225	poundforce	lbf
kPa	kilopascals	0.145	poundforce per square inch	lbf/in^2

Appendix B

GLOSSARY

SWGFAST (Scientific Working Group on Friction Ridge Analysis, Study and Technology)
Document #19
Standard Terminology of Friction Ridge Examination 1
(Latent/Tenprint)

ACE-V The acronym for a scientific method: Analysis, Comparison, Evaluation, and Verification (see individual terms).

AFIS The acronym for Automated Fingerprint Identification System, a generic term for a fingerprint matching, storage, and retrieval system.

Analysis The first step of the ACE-V method. The assessment of an impression to determine suitability for comparison.

APIS The acronym for Automated Palmprint Identification System, a generic term for a palmprint (or complete friction ridge exemplar) matching, storage, and retrieval system.

Arch—plain A pattern type in which the friction ridges enter on one side of the impression and flow, or tend to flow, out the other side with a rise or wave in the center.

Arch—tented A pattern type that possesses either an angle, an upthrust, or two of the three basic characteristics of the loop.

Artifact:
  1. Any distortion or alteration not in the original friction ridge impression, produced by an external agent or action.
  2. Any information not present in the original object or image, inadvertently introduced by image capture, processing, compressions, transmission, display, or printing.

Bias See cognitive bias, confirmation bias, and contextual bias.

Bifurcation The point at which one friction ridge divides into two friction ridges.

Blind verification The independent examination of one or more friction ridge impressions at any stage of the ACE process by another competent examiner who is provided with no, or limited, contextual information and has no expectation or knowledge of the determinations or conclusions of the original examiner.

Bridge A connecting friction ridge between, and generally at right angles to, parallel running friction ridges.

Characteristics Distinctive details of the friction ridges, including Level 1, 2, and 3 details (also known as features).

Cognitive bias The effect of perceptual or mental processes on the reliability and validity of one's observations and conclusions.

Comparison The second step of the ACE-V method. The observation of two or more impressions to determine the existence of discrepancies, dissimilarities, or similarities.

Competency Possessing and demonstrating the requisite knowledge, skills, and abilities to successfully perform a specific task.

Complete friction ridge exemplars A systematic recording of all friction ridge details appearing on the palmar sides of the hands. This includes the extreme sides of the palms, joints, tips, and sides of the fingers (also known as major case prints).

Complex examinations The encountering of uncommon circumstances during an examination (e.g., the existence of high distortion, low quality or quantity, the possibility of simultaneity, or conflicts among examiners).

Conclusion A determination made during the evaluation stage of ACE-V, including individualization, inconclusive, and exclusion.

Confirmation bias The tendency to search for data or interpret information in a manner that supports one's preconceptions.

Conflict A difference of determinations or conclusions that becomes apparent during, or at the end of, an examination.

Consensus determination or conclusion An agreement reflecting the collective judgment of a group of examiners trained to competency when making determinations or conclusions with respect to one or more impressions.

Consultation A significant interaction between examiners regarding one or more impressions in question.

Contextual bias The effect of information or outside influences on the evaluation and interpretation of data.

Core:
1. The approximate center of a fingerprint pattern.
2. A specific formation within a fingerprint pattern, defined by classification systems such as Henry.

Delta The point on a friction ridge at or nearest to the point of divergence of two type lines, located at or directly in front of the point of divergence. Also known as a triradius.

Deviation:
1. A change in friction ridge path.
2. An alteration or departure from a documented policy or standard procedure.

Discrepancy The presence of friction ridge detail in one impression that does not exist in the corresponding area of another impression (compare with dissimilarity).

Dissimilarity A difference in appearance between two friction ridge impressions (compare with discrepancy).

Dissociated ridges:
1. Disrupted, rather than continuous, friction ridges.
2. An area of friction ridge units that did not form into friction ridges, generally due to a genetic abnormality.

Distortion Variances in the reproduction of friction skin caused by factors such as pressure, movement, force, and contact surface.

Dot An isolated friction ridge unit whose length approximates its width in size.

Edgeoscopy:
1. Study of the morphological characteristics of friction ridges.
2. Contour or shape of the edges of friction ridges.

Elimination prints Exemplars of friction ridge skin detail of persons known to have had legitimate access to an object or location.

Enclosure A single friction ridge that bifurcates and rejoins after a short course and continues as a single friction ridge.

Ending ridge A single friction ridge that terminates within the friction ridge structure.

Erroneous exclusion The incorrect determination that two areas of friction ridge impressions did not originate from the same source.

Erroneous individualization The incorrect determination that two areas of friction ridge impressions originated from the same source.

Error A conclusion reached by an examiner that contradicts the mating status of two impressions and therefore is probably wrong (compare with nonconsensus decision).

Evaluation The third step of the ACE-V method, wherein an examiner assesses the value of the details observed during the analysis and the comparison steps and reaches a conclusion.

Exclusion The determination by an examiner that there is sufficient quality and quantity of detail in disagreement to conclude that two areas of friction ridge impressions did not originate from the same source.

Exemplars The prints of an individual, associated with a known or claimed identity, deliberately recorded electronically, by ink, or by another medium (also known as known prints).

False-negative rate (FNR) The proportion of the comparisons between mated prints that result in an erroneous exclusion conclusion.

False-positive rate (FPR) The proportion of the comparisons between nonmated prints that result in an erroneous individualization conclusion.

Features Distinctive details of the friction ridges, including Level 1, 2, and 3 details (also known as characteristics).

Fingerprint An impression of the friction ridges of all or any part of the finger.

Focal points:
1. In classification, the core(s) and the delta(s) of a fingerprint.
2. Another term for target group.

Friction ridge A raised portion of the epidermis on the palmar or plantar skin, consisting of one or more connected ridge units.

Friction ridge detail (morphology) An area comprised of the combination of ridge flow, ridge characteristics, and ridge structure.

Friction ridge examiner A person who analyzes, compares, evaluates, and verifies friction ridge impressions.

Friction ridge unit A single section of ridges containing one pore.

Furrows The valleys or depressions between friction ridges.

Galton details A term referring to friction ridge characteristics (also known as minutiae) attributed to the research of English fingerprint pioneer, Sir Francis Galton.

Ground truth Definitive knowledge of the actual source of an impression.

Henry classification An alpha-numeric system of fingerprint classification named after Sir Edward Richard Henry used for filing, searching, and retrieving tenprint records.

IAFIS The acronym for Integrated Automated Fingerprint Identification System, the FBI's national AFIS.

Identification:
1. See individualization.
2. In some forensic disciplines, this term denotes the similarity of class characteristics.

Impression A friction ridge detail deposited on a surface.

Incipient ridge A friction ridge not fully developed that may appear shorter and thinner than fully developed friction ridges.

Inconclusive The determination by an examiner that there is neither sufficient agreement to individualize, nor sufficient disagreement to exclude.

Individualization The determination by an examiner that there is sufficient quality and quantity of detail in agreement to conclude that two friction ridge impressions originated from the same source.

Joint (of the finger) The hinged area that separates segments of the finger.

Known prints (finger, palm, foot) The prints of an individual, associated with a known or claimed identity, deliberately recorded electronically, by ink, or by another medium (also known as exemplars).

Latent print:
1. The transferred impression of a friction ridge detail that is not readily visible.
2. A generic term used for an unintentionally deposited friction ridge detail.

Level 1 detail Friction ridge flow, pattern type, and general morphological information.

Level 2 detail Individual friction ridge paths and associated events, including minutiae.

Level 3 detail Friction ridge dimensional attributes, such as width, edge shapes, and pores.

Lift An adhesive or other medium used to transfer a friction ridge impression from a substrate.

Loop A pattern type in which one or more friction ridges enter upon one side, recurve, touch or pass an imaginary line between delta and core, and flow out, or tend to flow out, on the same side the friction ridges entered. Types include left slant loops, in which the pattern flows to the left in the impression; right slant loops, in which the pattern flows to the right in the impression; radial loops, in which the pattern flows in the direction of the radius bone of the forearm (toward the thumb); and ulnar loops, in which the pattern flows in the direction of the ulna bone of the forearm (toward the little finger).

Major case print A systematic recording of the friction ridge detail appearing on the palmar sides of the hands. This includes the extreme sides of the palms, joints, tips, and sides of the fingers (also known as complete friction ridge exemplars).

Mark A term commonly used in the United Kingdom and some Commonwealth countries to designate a latent print.

Mated impressions Impressions intentionally collected to originate from the same source and used for the purpose of measuring error rates.

Matrix The substance that is deposited or removed by the friction ridge skin when making an impression.

Minutiae Events along a ridge path, including bifurcations, ending ridges, and dots (also known as Galton details).

Missed exclusion The failure to make an exclusion when in fact the friction ridge impressions are nonmated (includes false positive, nonconsensus inconclusive, and nonconsensus no value).

Missed individualization The failure to make an individualization when in fact both friction ridge impressions are mated (includes false negative, nonconsensus inconclusive, and nonconsensus no value).

Negative predictive value (NPV) The proportion of exclusion determinations that are correct.

NGI The acronym for Next Generation Identification, the updated version of IAFIS.

Nonconsensus determinations of no value Decisions of no value that conflict with the consensus.

Nonconsensus determination of suitability When an examiner's determination of suitability does not concur with the consensus. Suitability determinations include nonconsensus no value and nonconsensus value decisions.

Nonconsensus determination of value Decisions of value that conflict with the consensus.

Nonconsensus exclusion conclusion When an examiner reaches a decision of exclusion that conflicts with the consensus, exclusive of false negative errors.

Nonconsensus inconclusive When an examiner reaches a decision of inconclusive that conflicts with the consensus, exclusive of false positive and negative errors.

Nonconsensus individualization conclusion When an examiner reaches a decision of individualization that conflicts with the consensus, exclusive of false positive errors.

Nonmated impressions Impressions intentionally collected to originate from different sources and used for the purpose of measuring error rates.

Original image An accurate replica (pixel for pixel) of the primary image.

Palmprint An impression of the friction ridges of all or any part of the palmar surface of the hand.

Pattern classification A subdivision of pattern type, defined by classification systems such as Henry or National Crime Information Center (NCIC) classifications.

Pattern type A fundamental pattern of the ridge flow: arch, loop, and whorl. Arches are subdivided into plain and tented arches; loops are subdivided into radial and ulnar loops; whorls are subdivided into plain whorls, double loops, pocket loops, and accidental whorls.

Phalanx/Phalange:
1. A bone of the finger or toe.
2. Sometimes used to refer to a segment of a finger.

Poroscopy A study of the size, shape, and arrangement of pores.

Positive predictive value (PPV) The proportion of individualization decisions that are correct.

Primary image The first recording of an image onto media.

Proficiency The ongoing demonstration of competency.

Quality The clarity of information contained within a friction ridge impression.

Quantity The amount of information contained within a friction ridge impression.

Ridge flow:
1. The direction of one or more friction ridges.
2. A component of a Level 1 detail.

Ridge path:
1. The course of a single friction ridge.
2. A component of a Level 2 detail.

Ridge unit See friction ridge unit.

Segment (of the finger) The proximal, medial, or distal section of the finger.

Short ridge A single friction ridge beginning, traveling a short distance, and then ending.

Simultaneous impression Two or more friction ridge impressions from the same hand or foot deposited concurrently.

Source An area of friction ridge skin from an individual from which an impression originated.

Spur A bifurcation with one short friction ridge branching off a longer friction ridge.

Stand-alone A segment of a simultaneous impression that has sufficient information to arrive at a conclusion of individualization, independent of other impressions within the aggregate.

Substrate The surface upon which a friction ridge impression is deposited.

Sufficiency The product of the quality and quantity of the objective data under observation (e.g., friction ridge, crease, and scar features).

Sufficient The determination that there is sufficiency in a comparison to reach a conclusion at the evaluation stage.

Suitable The determination that there is sufficiency in an impression to be of value for further analysis or comparison.

Target group A distinctive group of ridge features (and their relationships) that can be recognized.

Technical review A review of notes, documents, and other data that forms the basis for a scientific conclusion (see *ASCLD-LAB 2008 Manual*).

Tenprint:
1. A generic reference to examinations performed on intentionally recorded friction ridge impressions.
2. A controlled recording of an individual's available fingers using ink, electronic imaging, or other medium.

Tolerance   The amount of variation in appearance of friction ridge features to be allowed during a comparison, should a corresponding print be made available.

Trifurcation   The point at which one friction ridge divides into three friction ridges.

Type lines   The two innermost friction ridges associated with a delta that parallel, diverge, and surround, or tend to surround, the pattern area.

Verification   The independent application of the ACE process as utilized by a subsequent examiner to either support or refute the conclusions of the original examiner; this may be conducted as blind verification. Verification may be followed by some level of review as specified by agency policy.

Whorl—accidental:
1. A pattern type consisting of the combination of two different types of patterns (excluding the plain arch) with two or more deltas.
2. A pattern type that possesses some of the requirements for two or more different types of patterns.
3. A pattern type that conforms to none of the definitions of a pattern.

Whorl—central pocket loop   A pattern type that has two deltas and at least one friction ridge that makes, or tends to make, one complete circuit, which may be spiral, oval, circular, or any variant of a circle. An imaginary line drawn between the two deltas must not touch or cross any recurring friction ridges within the inner pattern area.

Whorl—double loop   A pattern type that consists of two separate loop formations with two separate and distinct sets of shoulders and two deltas.

Whorl—plain   A fingerprint pattern type that consists of one or more friction ridges that make, or tend to make, a complete circuit with two deltas between which, when an imaginary line is drawn, at least one recurring friction ridge within the inner pattern area is cut or touched.

Revision Table

Version Effective Start Effective End Posted Archived Change

3.1 02/11/11 11/16/12 09/04/12 11/16/12 Added in terms from new documents

4.0 11/16/12 N/A 11/24/12 N/A No change to content

Reformatted (start of new version number)

4.1 03/14/13 N/A 04/27/13 N/A Change in definition of "original image"

Appendix C

ALPHABETICAL LIST OF PROCESSES

Acid yellow 7
Amido black 10B (Methanol)
Amido black 10B (Aqueous)
Ardrox
Ashley's reagent
Basic red 28
Basic yellow 40
Coomassie brilliant blue R250
Crowle's double stain
Crystal violet
Cyanoacrylate fuming
DAB
Dental stone cast
DFO
Dye stain
Fluorescein
Fluorescent dye pink
Forensic light sources
Heat/flame particulates
Iodine fuming
IND (1,2-indanedione)
Leucocrystal violet
Lifting materials
Liquid gun blue
Luminol
MBD
M-star
Ninhydrin
Physical developer
Photo
Powders and particulates
Potassium thiocyanate
RAM

Rhodamine 6G aqueous
Rhodamine 6G methanol
RTX
Safranin-O
Silicone rubber casting
Silver nitrate
Small particle reagent
Sticky side powder
Sudan black
Tape-Glo
Thermal paper destaining solution
TMB
Wetwop
Zinc chloride

Index

Printed and bound by CPI Group (UK) Ltd, Croydon, CR0 4YY

08/06/2025

01896871-0001